Church, World, and Kingdom

The Eucharistic Foundation of Alexander Schmemann's Pastoral Theology

William C. Mills

D1529256

HillenbrandBooks

Chicago / Mundelein, Illinois

Nihil Obstat
Very Reverend Daniel
A. Smilanic, JCD
Vicar for Canonical Services
Archdiocese of Chicago
July 31, 2012

Imprimatur
Reverend Monsignor
John F. Canary, STL, DMIN
Vicar General
Archdiocese of Chicago
July 31, 2012

CHURCH, WORLD, AND KINGDOM: THE Eucharistic FOUNDATION OF ALEXANDER SCHMEMANN'S PASTORAL THEOLOGY © 2012 Archdiocese of Chicago: Liturgy Training Publications, 3949 South Racine Avenue, Chicago IL 60609; 1-800-933-1800, fax 1-800-933-7094, e-mail orders@ ltp.org. All rights reserved. See our website at www.LTP.org.

Hillenbrand Books is an imprint of Liturgy Training Publications (LTP) and the Liturgical Institute at the University of Saint Mary of the Lake (USML). The imprint is focused on contemporary and classical theological thought concerning the liturgy of the Catholic Church. Available at bookstores everywhere, through LTP by calling 1-800-933-1800, or visiting www.LTP.org. Further information about the **Hillenbrand Books** publishing program is available from the University of Saint Mary of the Lake/ Mundelein Seminary, 1000 East Maple Avenue, Mundelein, IL 60060 (847-837-4542), on the web at www.usml.edu/liturgicalinstitute, or e-mail litinst@usml.edu.

Printed in USA

Cover image © unknown, courtesy of Rev. William C. Mills.

Library of Congress Control Number: 2012940117

978-1-59525-038-4

HCWK

ALEXANDER SCHMEMANN
1921-1983
Memory Eternal

"Remember your leaders, those who spoke the word of God to you;
consider the outcome of their way of life, and imitate their faith."
—Hebrews 13:7

Contents

Preface

This book is a survey of the pastoral theology of the late Eastern Orthodox theologian Alexander Schmemann (1921-1983), who was a world-renowned priest, pastor, professor, seminary dean, theologian, speaker, and author. His life was devoted to the liturgical renewal and revival within the Eastern Orthodox Church, especially the Orthodox Church in America. Likewise, Schmemann's theological legacy has influenced all levels of Church life. His books, articles, essays, and sermons are known worldwide and have been translated into numerous languages and referenced by theologians in the East and the West, while at the same time serving as a general introduction to the Orthodox Christian faith and practice.[1]

Schmemann's most important contribution to theology is his emphasis on the Eucharist in the life and practice of the Church. His writings together with his lectures and sermons, reflect his passion for the Eucharist not only as an academic subject for study and reflection, but function as the formative factor for theological inquiry; for Schmemann, the Scriptures, doctrine, faith, teachings, practices, and prayers of the Church are expressed and fully realized in the Eucharistic gathering. One can see his life-long interest in the Eucharist throughout his writings, especially in his recently-published memoirs, his sermons from Radio Liberty, and his magnum opus *The Eucharist*.[2]

Yet implicit in his writings one can find rich commentary regarding the pastoral nature of the liturgy, what the Roman Catholic theologian Josef Jungmann and others have called pastoral liturgy.[3] Liturgy is deeply pastoral in that the Church's worship invites the

---

1. Paul Garrett ed. "Fr. Alexander Schmemann: A Chronological Bibliography" *St. Vladimir's Theological Quarterly* 28 (1984), 11-26. See also the web page dedicated to Schmemann's memory at www.schmemann.org.

2. For over thirty years Schmemann taped a weekly radio program called *Sunday Talks* hosted on the New York City based Radio Liberty program which was produced by Boris Shub. These talks were eventually broadcasted to the former Soviet Union as well as other Eastern European countries. Other Russian thinkers such as Vladimir Weidle, Victor Frank, and Gaito Gazdanov also hosted programs. For more information about the history of Radio Liberty see hooferfl.edu/rlexhibit/people-other-schmeann.php.

3. See Jungmann's essay titled "The Pastoral Idea in the History of the Liturgy" and Dom Olivier Rousseau's essay "Pastoral Liturgy and the Eastern Liturgies" in *The Assisi Papers:*

faithful around both Word and table in order to be in communion with one another and with the living God. The faithful are then sent back into the world to bring the peace, love, and joy of the Kingdom to the whole world. However the entire liturgical structure including the fast and festal periods, the sacraments of Baptism and marriage all help to form and shape the worshipping community into the Body of Christ, the Church. It is through liturgical worship where persons become members of this new messianic community whose head is Christ. Schmemann did not envision pastoral theology as a separate subject for study, something other or in addition to liturgy, but that pastoral theology and liturgy were intimately connected; that according to Schmemann, pastoral theology needs to be understood as a unique and important area of theology and that it is the Eucharist which is the source for reflecting on pastoral theology. This book shows how the Church can return to the wellspring of the liturgy in order to reform pastoral theology in both the academy and the Church.

The commentary in *Church, World, and Kingdom* is presented in a wide theological and ecumenical context and presents a well-rounded discussion on pastoral theology within the context of the liturgy. My formulation and explanation of pastoral theology utilizes an expanded theological vocabulary and ecumenical understanding of how we should speak about pastoral theology and its place within the Church. I provide a new grammar or way that we speak about pastoral theology, a language that is reflective not only of the writings of Alexander Schmemann, but of the Eastern theological tradition as a whole.

Furthermore, since Schmemann's life and work was deeply influenced by his experience with the Roman Catholic Liturgical Movement in Europe, especially in France, he was inspired by the work of L. Bouyer, J. Daniélou, and G. Dix among others, and was also an Orthodox observer at the proceedings of Vatican II. I have presented Schmemann's thought within the larger framework of the liturgical reforms and renewal of Vatican II, especially with consideration to *Sacrosanctum Concilium*, *Lumen Gentium*, as well as some of the post-conciliar documents such as *Mane Nobiscum Domine* and *Orientale Lumen* which have much affinity with the liturgical theology in the Eastern Church. Coming from an Eastern theological

Proceedings of the First International Congress of Pastoral Liturgy (Collegeville, MN: The Liturgical Press, 1957).

background, I have been inspired by much of what the late John Paul II has said about the richness of Eastern theology and have also included Schmemann's thought within the context of *Orientale Lumen*, which touches upon the theological and liturgical heritage in the East.

Likewise, my work on this book has been deeply influenced by my experience in theological ecumenism, especially with the Pastor-Theologian Program at the Center of Theological Inquiry at Princeton University. Gathering regularly with pastors from diverse Christian backgrounds for prayer, Bible study, and theological discussion, has provided me with the opportunity to further reflect on the ecumenical nature of theology, especially pastoral theology. This ecumenical work has enlarged my theological vocabulary and shaped the way I envision pastoral theology as being both pastoral and theological, which is not always how pastoral theology is discussed in seminaries and graduate schools of theology. The fact that groups of pastors take the time in order to think and reflect on theological issues together in a group setting has become the fertile soil from which ideas have blossomed for this book. I would hope pastors who read *Church, World, and Kingdom* would find it conducive for small group discussions and reflections on the pastoral nature of liturgy and how we as pastors can draw from the deep wells of our liturgical worship to find some answers to our contemporary theological questions and problems.

What does a priest from an Eastern Orthodox theological tradition have to say to a predominately Roman Catholic audience? Given the fact that Schmemann himself was deeply influenced by the Roman Catholic Liturgical Movement in France and then later in the United States and was one of the pioneers in the ecumenical discussions and debates in North America, I too envision this book as a real dialogue between both East and West so that we can learn from one another, especially regarding our common liturgical and sacramental heritage. In *Orientale Lumen*, John Paul II emphasized the rich theological and liturgical tradition of the Eastern Church, which has been preserved in liturgical worship:

> Certain features of the spiritual and theological tradition, common to the various Churches of the East mark their sensitivity to the forms taken by the transmission of the Gospel in Western lands. The Second

Vatican Council summarized them as follows, "Everyone knows with what love the Eastern Christians celebrate the sacred liturgy, especially the Eucharistic mystery, source of the Church's life and pledge of future glory. In this mystery the faithful, united with their bishops, have access to God the Father through the Son, the Word made flesh who suffered and was glorified, in the outpouring of the Holy Spirit. And so, made "sharers of the divine nature" (2 Peter 1:4) they enter into communion with the most holy Trinity. These features describe the Eastern outlook of the Christian. His or her goal is participation in the divine nature through communion with the mystery of the Holy Trinity.[4]

John Paul II emphasizes the notion of true participation in the life of the Trinity in liturgical worship. That it is through the participation in the sacramental life of the Church, through receiving Holy Communion, confessing sins to the priest, and through the other sacraments, that one is able to enter into the communal love of God. The faithful then share this common love with those people around them, mirroring the love and self-sacrifice of the Trinity; Father, Son, and Holy Spirit. I hope that this book can create a bridge between East and West in terms of how we formulate our understanding of pastoral theology and our work in the wider Church. Alexander Schmemann was committed to open dialogue and discussion with his Catholic colleagues and I hope that this book is a small contribution to the continued theological discussion.

I also hope that non-Catholics will benefit from reading Schmemann's thoughts on pastoral theology since many scholars and theologians from other Christian traditions continue to be inspired, encouraged, and renewed by Schmemann's writings.

A brief note regarding the title of this book is needed. Throughout his writings, Schmemann always maintained clear theological connections between the Church, which is the community of baptized Christians living in the world and the Kingdom of Heaven, which is most clearly manifested in the Church's worship, the Eucharistic Divine Liturgy. Likewise, there cannot be any division between the Church and the world since Christ himself told his disciples to be in the world but not of it.[5] While on the one hand the

---

4. *Orientale Lumen* (OL), 6.

5. This theme of openness to the world is seen in numerous Orthodox writings, see especially Paul Evdokimov, in In the World, of the Church, Michael Plekon and Alex Vinogradov,

Gospels portray the world as being in darkness, however, it is in this darkness that God's Son Jesus Christ manifested his light, power, and glory. At the end of his earthly life Jesus sent out his disciples into this world in order to continue his preaching and teaching ministry. In other words, the Apostles were sent into the world to herald in the Kingdom of God. The Church, then, is the physical or visual expression of God's Kingdom, the place where we hear the Gospel proclaimed, where people are adopted as children of God through the sacrament of Baptism, and where we receive Christ himself through the common elements of bread and wine. The Church is where we share our joys, pains, and sorrows, bearing with one another and helping one another in life. At the conclusion of the liturgy we are invited to return back to our homes, families, and workplaces in order to live out our faith in God among the people around us. Therefore, as members of the Church of God we are also living for the Kingdom of God in this world until the Lord returns.

Taking Schmemann's lead I have adopted these three pillars: Church, world, and Kingdom, as the pillars on which my book stands. These three pillars also form the three poles of pastoral theology that is expressed in the Church, for the life of the world, and living for the Kingdom of God:

> And thus: the world, the Church, the kingdom. All of God's creation, all salvation, all fulfillment. Heaven on earth. One voice and one heart, one glorification and singing of the all honorable name: of Father, and of the Son, and of the Holy Spirit, now and ever and unto ages of ages. Amen. Here is the essence of this great, crowning prayer; here is the ultimate supplication of the eucharist, united around the Lamb of God, in Christ—the entire spiritual world, beginning with the Theotokos and the saints and ending with all—be all things to all men. This is what we are summoned to behold, to recognize, to perceive each time the eucharist is celebrated. In this we must immerse our whole consciousness, all our love, all our desire, before approaching "our immortal King and God."[6]

---

translators and editors,(Crestwood, NY: St. Vladimir's Seminary Press, 2001), p. 61-94. Other Orthodox authors such as Anton Kartashev and Sergius Bulgakov speak of "Churchifying" the culture and society. In other words, rather than fleeing the world, Christians are called to embrace the culture around us, bringing the light and truth of the Gospel to the world.

6. Alexander Schmemann, *The Eucharist*, translated by Paul Kachur (Crestwood, NY: St. Vladimir's Seminary Press, 1988), 239.

For Schmemann the Eucharist is the source and summit not only of theology but for the entire Church. Throughout all his writings Schmemann emphasizes that the Eucharist is firmly rooted in the Church, offered for the life of the world, whose destination is the Kingdom of Heaven. Ultimately, the Eucharist must be missionary since we gather together to share communion and break bread but we are then sent out to share our joy of the Kingdom with the whole world, which is a continuation of the ministry of Jesus' disciples, "Go, therefore, and make disciples of all nations, baptizing them in the name of the Father, and of the Son, and of the holy Spirit, teaching them to observe all that I have commanded you. And behold, I am with you always, until the end of the age" (Mt. 28:19-20). "Those who accepted his message were baptized, and about three thousand persons were added that day. They devoted themselves to the teaching of the Apostles and to the communal life, to the breaking of the bread and to the prayers" (Acts 2:41-42). Thus, Schmemann draws on the Eucharist as a source for pastoral reflection in that ultimately pastoral theology is to bring parishioners into an encounter with the living God and then send them back out into the world in order to live a grace filled life.

This study on Schmemann is the only one that is primarily devoted to Schmemann's pastoral theology. While there are numerous essays, articles, and monographs that deal with other aspects of his theology, especially his liturgical theology and ecclesiology, there are no resources currently available that focus on his thoughts on pastoral ministry.

Finally, and most importantly, *Church, World, and Kingdom* contains previously unpublished material from Alexander Schmemann's archives that are currently housed at the Fr. Georges Florovsky library at St. Vladimir's Orthodox Theological Seminary. I was given exclusive permission to use his archival material for my dissertation research. This new research has shed light on the importance of the liturgical and Eucharistic context for ministry, especially highlighting the spiritual, practical, and theological preparation of ordained clergy as well as the pitfalls of clericalism and the general ministry of the entire Body of Christ, both clergy and laity. This book includes material which will provide an important contribution to theological scholarship.

As with any project of this magnitude I am grateful to a number of persons without whom I could not have accomplished such a task. First and foremost I must thank my doctoral committee who guided me along the winding and narrow paths of academia. I am especially grateful to my academic advisor Lawrence J. Ryan, PHD, who is the perfect mentor: patient, kind, gentle, but always firm and inspiring. Likewise, I am grateful to the other members of my doctoral committee, Daniel Findykian, PHD, Stephen Plumlee, PHD, Andrew Purves, PHD, Rich Douglas, PHD, Abbot Placid Solari, OSB, PHD, and Kevin Sharpe, PHD. Their comments and criticisms throughout the writing process allowed me to maintain proper perspective and coherence. I would also like to thank Eleana Silk and the library staff of the Fr. Georges Florovsky Library at the campus of St. Vladimir's Orthodox Theological Library for their research assistance and help with obtaining references. Likewise, Kevin Thornton and the editorial board at Hillenbrand Books have been very generous, always providing support and guidance throughout the editorial process.

A word of thanks is due to my colleagues and friends, Frs. Michael Plekon and Stephen Hrycyniak. Their support and encouragement throughout this writing project was most welcome, especially during long bouts of writer's block. Stephen's encouragement in publishing and Michael's expertise in the area of modern Orthodox theology and the Russian religious renaissance greatly contributed to this project, especially as I considered Schmemann's theological background and theological formation.

Finally, I am always inspired by the everlasting patience, love, and generosity of my beloved wife Taisia and daughters Hannah and Emma who sacrificed precious time away from me so I could finish this project. I could not have accomplished any of this without their constant prayers, support, smiles, and hugs; because of them I have much to be thankful for.

Part 1

Foundations of
Pastoral Theology

Chapter 1

Pastoral Theology Today: People and Praxis

Before entering directly into a discussion of Alexander Schmemann's thoughts on pastoral theology, it is important to understand his immediate background and theological context. A brief overview of the major issues and concerns within the field of pastoral theology is important in order to understand Schmemann's unique contribution to this area of theology. First we will review several problematic areas of pastoral theology, or major theological divisions; then we will explore how Schmemann seemed to address these concerns by looking at the sacramental practices of the Church.

Throughout the 20th century, scholars and theologians have debated the nature and purpose of pastoral theology. In many ways, the field of pastoral theology and ministry has suffered from what some people consider to be an identity crisis. In some seminaries and graduate schools of theology, pastoral theology has been relegated to the practical or everyday concerns of parish life such as parish administration, fundraising, or counseling, which have somewhat replaced the more traditional theological courses such as Scripture, liturgy, Church history, and homiletics: areas of study that were once known as the jewels of theology. This is quite unfortunate, since these seminaries are producing pastors who may be able to raise funds for a new Church building but have difficulty speaking on theological subjects such as Christology, Church history, or ecumenism.[1]

---

1. This situation of course is not the norm in many Eastern Orthodox or Roman Catholic seminaries. However, if one reviews the course offerings and programs of some non-Roman Catholic seminaries one would see many courses such as public speaking and fundraising and few courses in what would be considered traditional or classical theology.

Furthermore, some theological academies demand skills for their pastors so that they can meet the changing needs of modern culture and society. Pastors are called to be evangelists and missionaries, caring for the poor and the needy, as well as serving as the chief administrative executive for the congregation. Pastors are continuously under numerous demands to focus solely on parish administration in order to keep up with shifting technological and cultural concerns rather than focus on their calling to be shepherds of Christ's Church, as noted by the pastoral theologian Marva J. Dawn, "Pastors are burdened with so much 'administrivia' that they have no time to focus, as Acts 6:4 suggests, on prayer and the ministry of the Word. (This change is indicated by the fact that we call their places of work 'the office' instead of 'the study.')"[2]

Dawn is not alone in her assessment of some contemporary seminary curricula. Others have noted that the shifting demands of contemporary parish life—such as inter-faith marriages, new contemporary forms of worship, and social outreach programs—have put increased demands on seminary faculty to teach students pragmatic and practical tasks for their students, rather than to have them well versed in the classic texts of theology.[3] This new emphasis on administrative activity can often overshadow pastoral care. Very often pastoral care is reduced to situational care or pastoral triage, rather than helping to foster or inspire a person's faith, or bring them into contact with the living God:

> The primal interest of the psychologically oriented pastoral care is to release people from their anxieties and bring them in an emotionally balanced situation. Since it does not presuppose that all the members of the Church need to grow in faith and love, it does not pay attention to the guidance of all the members of the Church towards the fullness of the Christian life but only to those of them who are in crisis situations. Therefore it becomes a "crisis oriented" pastoral care. It does not for example, teach a Christian how to pray or how to face a difficulty in his emotional life. It tends to be also a "situational" pastoral care, responding to the situation by taking inspirations only from the given situation and not from the also given Word of God. It is rather anthropocentric than

---

2. Marva J. Dawn, *Reaching Out Without Dumbing Down: A Theology of Worship for This Urgent Time* (Grand Rapids, MI: Eerdmans, 1995), 44.

3. Henri Nouwen, *Creative Ministry* (New York: Doubleday, 1971), iii.

theocentric. At this point one can realize the influence of secularism on the movement as on the whole life of the Church.[4]

George Kapsanis' above reflection on pastoral care was made in response to the then-growing role of Clinical Pastoral Education (CPE), which originated from the work and research of Anton Boisen and Seward Hiltner.[5] Both Boisen and Hiltner emphasized a clinical model of pastoral care, an anthropocentric one that focused on specific human situations, looking at the parishioner or client as a living human document, rather than focusing on the person's relationship with God, which is a more theocentric model. There are many wonderful benefits of CPE programs, which teach students to cultivate their listening skills and provide them with extensive training in compassion and care-giving in a safe environment. However, these pastoral skills cannot replace the lifeblood of the Church, which is liturgical worship and prayer.

The CPE movement is not without its critics. Many have questioned why professionally and scientifically trained counselors would mix Christian faith with science.[6] However, Kapsanis' critique is noteworthy, since even back in 1967 he offered a prophetic challenge: "Pastoral care is at a crucial point in its development. It faces a dilemma: Will it reduce itself to a humanistic discipline or will it discover new possibilities and new methods within the faith and the theology of the Church?"[7]

Today, the tide is changing and scholars have started to redirect the conversation of pastoral theology to a more theological

---

4. George Kapsanis, "Pastoral Care in American Practice," *St. Vladimir's Theological Quarterly* 11 (1967): 207–211.

5. See Seward Hiltner, *Ferment in the Ministry* (Nashville: Abingdon, 1969); Hiltner, *Pastoral Counseling* (Nashville: Abingdon, 1949); and Hiltner, *Preface to Pastoral Theology* (Nashville: Abingdon, 1958). See also Donald Capps, *Life Cycle: Theory and Pastoral Care* (Philadelphia: Fortress, 1983).

6. This new professionalism among those in ministry has given rise to new ministerial guilds, such as the Academy of Parish Clergy. For more information on this particular group, see www.apclergy.org.

7. George Kapsanis, "Pastoral Care in American Practice," *St. Vladimir's Theological Quarterly* 11 (1967), 210. One of the problems that Kapsanis and Schmemann had concerning pastoral care was that in the early stages of the CPE movement, greater emphasis was placed on the counseling roles of new pastors. Schmemann makes several poignant remarks about pastoral counseling in general in *The Journals of Father Alexander Schmemann, 1973–1983* (Crestwood, NY: St. Vladimir Seminary Press, 2000), 14, 15, 106, 182, 332.

level. *Church, World, and Kingdom* is just one more voice in the chorus. The new conversation seems to be moving toward a more theocentric and Christocentric context, which is not only more scripturally sound, but is also expressed through the sacramental life of the Church. In this book—as in Schmemann's work—we mean that pastoral theology, in its very foundation, helps us realize that each and every member of this Body is important and special, and that we are all called to use our God-given talents for the building up of his Church. Since this model of pastoral theology is firmly rooted in the sacraments, especially the Eucharist, this will have affinity with Eastern Orthodox and Roman Catholic audiences.

Theologians in both East and West have also noted the theological reduction of pastoral theology that Kapsanis and others have talked about. Andrew Purves, Thomas Oden, Carl Volz, Aidan Kavanagh, Henri Nouwen, Alexander Schmemann, and Eugene Peterson have all called for a redirection in the modern conversation of pastoral theology, away from a clinical model to a more theologically-based one.[8] While these authors approach pastoral theology from different ecclesial backgrounds and theological disciplines, they affirm that the predominant focus of what is known today as pastoral ministry has displaced the theological root of pastoral ministry.[9] Some scholars have noted that within this contemporary model of pastoral theology there is little reflection on the importance of salvation, grace and sanctification, redemption and forgiveness of sins, and seeking union and communion with Christ.[10] According to the recent work of Andrew Purves, pastoral theology has lost its biblical and theological moorings:

> Pastoral work is concerned always with the gospel of God's redemption in and through Jesus Christ, no matter the problem that someone presents.

---

8. Thomas C. Oden, *Pastoral Theology: Essentials of Ministry.* (New York: Harper and Row, 1983); Eugene H. Peterson, *Under the Unpredictable Plant: An Exploration in Vocational Holiness* (Grand Rapids, MI: Eerdmans, 1992); Carl A. Volz, *Pastoral Life and Practice in the Early Church,* (Minneapolis, MN: Augsburg, 1990); Andrew Purves, *Pastoral Theology in the Classical Tradition* (Louisville, KY: Westminster John Knox Press, 2001); and Andrew Purves, *Reconstructing Pastoral Theology: A Christological Foundation* (Louisville, KY: Westminster John Knox Press, 2004). See also Philip L. Culbertson and Arthur Shippee, eds., *The Pastor: Readings From the Patristic Period* (Minneapolis, MN: Fortress, 1990).

9. Oden, *Pastoral Theology,* 4.

10. Ibid., 3.

> Pastoral work by definition connects the gospel story—the truths and
> realities of God's saving economy—with the actual lives and situations
> of people. Biblical and theological perspectives guide pastoral work, and
> these perspectives, properly rooted in the gospel of salvation, are discov-
> ered to be inherently pastoral . . . A relatively comfortable synthesis
> results in which pastoral theology, and, consequently, pastoral practice in
> the church, have become concerned largely with questions of meaning
> rather than truth, acceptable functioning rather than discipleship, and a
> concern for self-actualization and self-realization rather than salvation.[11]

Purves asserts that there are two guiding principles of pastoral
ministry, the Scriptures and theology, both of which have been lost in
the contemporary reflection and discussion of pastoral ministry today.
His thesis is that pastoral theology must be firmly rooted in the person
of Jesus Christ if it is going to be considered Christian pastoral theology.

Therefore, Jesus Christ should be the foundation for pastoral
theology, and is the one who leads us to knowledge of God, and the
one who bestows on us the gift of the Holy Spirit. Therefore, if
pastoral theology is not first and foremost based on the preaching and
teaching ministry of Jesus Christ, then it is simply reduced to another
helping profession where pastors are considered helpers rather than
pastors or shepherds.

Likewise, since Christians believe in the Trinity, they must
also accept and affirm that God is revealed as Trinity: Father, Son, and
Holy Spirit. The Trinity is a community of persons who share a fellowship of self-sacrificial love for one another. Therefore, pastoral theology
must be firmly rooted in the Christological and Trinitarian teachings
that are expressed and affirmed in the creedal formulas of the Church,
namely the Apostles' Creed and the Nicene-Constantinopolitan Creed,
the ones commonly shared by Catholic and Orthodox Christians.

Purves is correct in his understanding of the current identity
crisis regarding pastoral theology. Though he mentions the sacramental
or liturgical aspects of pastoral theology, he does not emphasize them.
In other words, he rightly affirms the need for a Christological and
Trinitarian basis for pastoral care, yet stops short of recognizing its
intimate connection with the Church's worship.

---

11. Ibid.

The Academy and the Church

Until quite recently, in many institutions, there has been a theological disconnect between formal academic theology and Church teaching.[12] Historically, theology was always viewed as service to the Church. The great theological doctors of the Church, John Chrysostom, Cyril of Jerusalem, Gregory the Great, Ambrose of Milan, Augustine of Hippo, and Gregory Nazianzen were pastors who regularly preached the Gospel, taught the faith, presided at the Eucharist, and administered their dioceses. These leaders were confessors of the faith, and helped to form and shape their local church. They were also active in their local communities as leaders and defenders of the poor, the orphaned, the widowed, and the destitute. Basil of Caeserea established one of the first mental hospitals in Byzantium, reminding people that the Church was first and foremost a place for healing. According to Basil, the Church had an important role to play in the healing of others, especially the sick and the suffering. Likewise, Chrysostom regularly preached about the importance of almsgiving and care for the poor, which is the duty of every Christian, not just the wealthy.[13] Chrysostom also devoted his ministry to encouraging other clergy in their ministry, especially with his famous *Six Books on the Priesthood*.[14] Gregory the Great wrote his *Pastoral Rule* to better assist clergy in governing their parishes and dioceses.[15] His *Pastoral Rule* is a textbook for pastoral care, full of wonderful reflections on the importance of spiritual guidance and direction, the role of the pastor in the community, and the importance of preaching and teaching the faith.

---

12. Wallace Alston, former director of the Center of Theological Inquiry, has stated that the Church's problem isn't the lack of programs and activity, but the clear disconnect between the theological schools and the parish Church. See Wallace M. Alston Jr. and Cynthia A. Jarvis, *The Power to Comprehend With All the Saints* (Grand Rapids, MI: Eerdmans, 2009), especially page xiv of the introduction, where Alston comments, "A striking fact about the church in our time is that where ministers pursue their calling as church theologians the church lives . . . and where they do not, the church tends to be trivialized and languishes. One might well document the fact that the crisis in the church parallels the loss of theological identity by the church and the shift in its understanding of the minister from that of the theologian to that of the chief executive officer."

13. See John Chrysostom, *On Wealth and Poverty*, trans. Catherine P. Roth (Crestwood, New York: St. Vladimir's Seminary Press, 1984).

14. John Chrysostom, *Six Books on the Priesthood*, trans. Graham Neville (Crestwood, New York: St. Vladimir's Seminary Press, 1984).

15. Gregory the Great, *St. Gregory the Great: Pastoral Care*, trans. Henry Davies (Mahwah, NJ: Newman Press, 1950).

These ancient pastors were well trained not only in theology but also in law, philosophy, classical rhetoric, and ethics, and they were conversant in topics including literature, the arts, culture, society, and politics. For these great *doctores ecclesiae*, the purpose of theology was the building up of the Body of Christ, or as Gregory Nazianzen wrote, "the scope of our art is to provide the soul with wings, to rescue it from the world and give it to God, and to watch over that which is His image, if it abides, to take it by the hand, if it is in danger, to restore it, if ruined, to make Christ to dwell in the heart by the Spirit: and, in short, to deify, and bestow heavenly bliss upon, one who belongs to the heavenly host."[16]

When these ancient pastoral theologians wrote extended theological treatises defending the Trinity or the divinity of Christ or sent letters to other clergy or spiritual children, they wrote them for the common good of the Church. In other words, they were not writing for one another's theological edification but for the good of the Christian community in times of theological crisis and doubt. Their sermons, pastoral letters, and writings were always meant for the Church: to encourage and admonish the faithful to embrace the cross of Christ in their daily lives. The ancients viewed pastoral care as the way to bring a person into greater communion with the ineffable God, who emptied himself to become what we are (Phil 2:5–11). Commenting on the theological and pastoral writings of Gregory Nazianzen, the patristic scholar Brian Daley has said:

> Christian pastoring is always theology first of all: speaking about the God revealed by Jesus, the God involved personally in created history as Father, Son, and Holy Spirit, the God who shapes us and draws us not just to know him, but to participate in his life. To speak rightly of God, to avoid the danger of self-promoting "babble" in our preaching, requires that the pastor's speech be unmistakably centered on the news of Jesus, divine and human, as it is contained in the scriptures, the rule of faith, and the church's confessions. Theology of any kind is always dialogue, bringing these traditional sources for speech about God into conversation with the scientific, philosophical, and cultural concerns of each new age. But the pastor who attempts to carry out his task of leadership or sacramental ministry or therapeutic engagement apart from this theological,

---

16. Gregory of Nazianzen, *Oration* 2.22, in Philip Schaff and Henry Ware, eds., *Nicene and Post-Nicene Fathers: Second Series* (Grand Rapids, MI: Eerdmans, 1989), 209.

kerygmatic center is like someone leading an expedition in the dark or operating without surgical training—the exercise soon becomes aimless and empty.[17]

However, for the past fifty years there has been a real divide between theology and the Church. Theology, which was once for the whole Christian community, has been relegated to the chosen few who hold academic chairs of theology in seminaries and graduate schools. Often those who live and work behind the walls of the academy write only for others within the theological guild. Theology was never meant to be a specialized subject in the humanities, but was for the salvation of souls and the building up of the Body of Christ.

Pastoral and theological disciplines have thus been placed in a situation where it is almost impossible for them to interact upon each other except sporadically and, as it were, anecdotally. When the theological academy allows the pastoral field into its structure, its presence there is usually encased by conditions that render it highly unlikely to affect the conventional theological disciplines. The pastoral field, in turn, brings these restrictions upon itself by going about its business of flushing out problems, but attempting to deal with them only by clinical and educational techniques, which often betray little—if any—understanding of, or correlation to, theological discipline.[18]

Kavanagh identifies a serious breach between the academic study of theology and the role of theology in the Church. A good example of this can be seen in some Orthodox seminaries, where few faculty members have actually pastored in a parish setting, and are therefore impervious to the pressures, strains, and life of a worshipping community—yet they are the ones who are training future clergy.

While parish administration and fundraising are important activities, they are not the central focus of pastoral care. The pastor's primary vocation is to make Christ present in the local worshipping community through regular preaching and teaching, through leading the congregation in prayer and worship, and through personal encounters.[19]

---

17. Brian E. Daley, "Saint Gregory of Nazianzus as Pastor and Theologian," in Michael Welker and Cynthia A. Jarvis, eds., *Loving God With Our Minds: The Pastor As Theologian: Essays in Honor of Wallace Alston* (Grand Rapids, MI: Eerdmans, 2004), 106.

18. Aidan Kavanagh, *On Liturgical Theology* (Collegeville, MN: Pueblo, 1984), 19.

19. Peterson, *Under the Unpredictable Plant*, 3.

A Theological Answer

One major solution to this modern pastoral challenge resides in a theological transformation and renewal for a deeper pastoral theology. According to the biblical and historical witness, the pastor is the spiritual leader of the congregation, and his primary function is to make Christ present in the worshipping community. The pastor engages in this holy activity through leading the congregation in prayer, proclaiming the Good News of the Gospel, reconciling the wayward, counseling and consoling the sick and suffering, and caring for the poor and destitute. However, all of the regular tasks of the priest flow from and lead to the Eucharistic table. When the priest leads the congregation in prayer and praise around the Lord's Table, he is leading them in their Eucharistic work, which Lutheran pastor and theologian Frank Senn has even called the people's work, a title of one of his books. Senn identifies worship as the central work of the people of God, returning to church each week to offer the liturgy in thanksgiving to God for everything that he has already accomplished in his Son Jesus.[20] Thus the pastor's main task is to become the hands and feet of Christ, leading the flock to a deeper communion with God.

Pastoral work therefore is deeply Christological, in that it is rooted in the person and ministry of Jesus Christ who has redeemed us through the blood of the cross and made us children of light and of the day. It is our faith in the person of Jesus Christ that gives us life. The Gospel according to John reminds us that Jesus is the way, the truth, and the life. For the Christian believer, Christ is the very foundation, source, and fountain from which we draw life, where we look for direction—and, ultimately, for our salvation. After the multiplication of loaves and fishes, Peter makes an affirmation of faith recorded only in the Gospel according to John, "Master, to whom shall we go? You have the words of eternal life. We have come to believe and are convinced that you are the Holy One of God" (Jn 6:68–69). Without Jesus Christ, pastoral theology is reduced to another form of self-help: one that may provide guidance, direction, and hope, but will not lead us to salvation. Our life in Christ is an essential component of faith, and we are called to abide or remain with him: "Remain in me, as I remain in you. Just as a branch cannot

---

20. Frank Senn, *The People's Work* (Minneapolis, MN: Augsburg Fortress, 2006).

bear fruit on its own unless it remains on the vine, so neither can you unless you remain in me. I am the vine, you are the branches. Whoever remains in me and I in him will bear much fruit, because without me you can do nothing. Anyone who does not remain in me will be thrown out like a branch and wither; people will gather them and throw them into a fire and they will be burned" (Jn 15:4–6).

Abiding with Christ also presupposes community. Christians cannot be Christians alone, but are always in a community. This community of faith is the gathering of Jesus' disciples who come together for prayer and praise, and who do the Lord's work in this world. The Scriptures provide many metaphors for this community, including a body, a building, and a flock. Christians are called to live out their lives with other people, always striving to serve and love their neighbor, which is the penultimate commandment from Jesus himself. When we are loving our neighbor, we are showing our love for God.

However our faith is not in Jesus alone, since Jesus was sent by God the Father, "In the beginning was the Word, and the Word was with God, and the Word was God. He was in the beginning with God. All things came to be through him, and without him nothing came to be. What came to be through him was life, and this life was the light of the human race" (Jn 1:1–4). While remaining God, totally other, God makes himself known to us through the person of his Son Jesus Christ.

Thus God reveals himself to us as a Trinity, a union of three persons, co-equal, co-ruling, who share a bond of love and fellowship. The Trinity, then, is the example for the Christian community: while we gather as a community of faith, we do not lose our individual identities or personalities, but share a common bond of love and fellowship. The Holy Trinity is a model for how we should live out our high calling as disciples of Christ. Likewise, the Trinity draws us to both the Word and the Table as we share our common prayer and praise to God, which is fulfilled in the Eucharistic sacrifice. Thus it is in the liturgy, the divine work of God's people, that we experience fully our unity of faith, love, and communion. It is also within the context of the liturgy that we may find an answer to the current challenges of pastoral theology.

A Liturgical Foundation for Theology

Our Christian faith requires more than formal academic discussions on Christology and Trinitarian theology; these must be lived out in our worship. It is through the prayers, hymns, feast days, fasting periods, and sacraments that we live out our faith as we are comforted, reproved, encouraged, and led to the Kingdom of Heaven. Thus the liturgy is the place where we encounter the Holy Trinity face to face: in both his life-giving Word and in the broken Body and spilled Blood, which is given to us for the life of the world and its salvation. It is primarily through regular worship that pastors are engaged in the pastoral care of their flocks:

> All pastoral work originates in this act of worship. Each Lord's Day the pastor speaks the invitational command, "Let us worship God." But the work does not terminate an hour later with the pronouncing of the benediction, for pastoral work also accompanies the people as they live out what they have heard and sung and said and believed in worship. Pastoral work takes place between Sundays, between the first and the eighth day, between the boundaries of creation and resurrection, between Genesis 1 and Revelation 21. Sunday worship establishes the life of the community of faith in and on the word of God; weekday pastoral work unfolds the implications in the ordinary lives of people as they work, love, suffer, grieve, play, learn, and grow in times of crisis and times of routine. Worship calls a congregation to attention before God's words, coordinates responses of praise and obedience, and then sends the people out into the community to live out the meaning of praise and obedience. But they are not only sent, they are accompanied, and pastoral work is the ministry of that accompaniment. Pastoral work begins at the Pulpit, the Font, the Table; it continues in the hospital room, the family room, the counseling room, the committee room. The pastor who leads people in worship is companion to those same people between acts of worship. . . .[21]

Pastoral work is as much a derivation from the Eucharist as preparation for it, for it helps those who have received into their bodies the spirit of life of Christ to realize that love in every detail of every relationship. The prayers offered at the Eucharistic table are continued in homes and

---

21. Eugene Peterson, *Five Smooth Stones for Pastoral Work* (Grand Rapids, MI: William Eerdmans, 1992), 19.

hospitals, in committee rooms and work tables. Pastoral work gives visibility to these continuities.[22]

Peterson is correct here in asserting that it is within the context of the weekly worship service that people offer their hurt, pain, brokenness, and suffering to the awesome God on high, and are filled and fed with the Bread of Life who is Christ himself come to nourish us with his life-giving Word, and broken Body, and spilled Blood. He comes as the prophet who reproves and corrects us, the shepherd who leads us, the physician who heals us, and the Bread of Life who feeds us. As the shepherd, Jesus accompanies his followers along the craggy path of life, leading us beside the still waters and showing us the Kingdom. Sometimes we—like sheep—go astray, yet Jesus goes and brings us back to that narrow path. Pastors need to take the lead of Christ himself, the Good Shepherd.

Peterson is one of the few scholars in the Western Church who has clearly identified the theological renewal of pastoral care, which is focused on the biblical witness of Scripture and lived out in the worship of the community of faith. The various Orthodox and Catholic churches would very much benefit from a new and vibrant focus on the pastoral nature of the liturgy. The link between pastoring and worship is not new. Chrysostom, Augustine, and Ambrose were just as fully at home alone in their studies as they were at the altar leading their congregations in regular times of worship and community prayer. Church historian Robert Louis Wilken draws attention to the ease at which these pastor-theologians envisioned their role in relation to the liturgy:

> By actions and words the liturgy engraved the communion of the saints on the minds and hearts of Christian thinkers. They praised God in the presence of others, and when they returned to their studies this company remained present. There is no intellectual elitism among the church fathers. Their thinking was not only nourished by the communal experience of the church, but also beholden to a community that reaches back in time and will exist in the future as a city whose purpose is to "worship the Lamb" (Rv 22:3). What they wrote in their books and essays they preached to their congregations, often in the same words. The liturgy drew bishops and faithful into shared public life whose central activity

---

22. Ibid., 63.

was the worship of the Triune God, and Christian thought developed in intimate connection with the church's life, her sacraments and practices, Scripture and creeds, martyrs and saints, and in the company of the whole host of heaven.[23]

The Church fathers lived the liturgy. Their pastoral work was centered on the liturgy of the Church, and their preaching and teaching were formed around the feasts and fasts of the Church.[24] The vast quantity of sermons and writings that have survived the centuries testify to the liturgical nature of their ministry. These ancient pastors clearly identified the connections among Scripture, theology, liturgy, and life. When they preached or taught in church, they were preaching the Gospel in the context of the liturgical gathering. In conducting catechetical classes, they were preparing their flock for reception into the Church of God and were thus leading their flock to a deeper understanding of the rites and rituals of the Church. When they wrote letters or theological treatises, they wrote them in order to teach an important aspect of the faith or to lead their clergy into an under-standing of the importance of their ministry. One only has to read a few pages of Gregory's *Pastoral Rule* or Chrysostom's *On the Priesthood* to see their devotion to the theological foundation of ministry. This book is one attempt to redirect the conversation to a renewal of the liturgical and sacramental focus of pastoral theology as it is expressed in the living liturgy of the Church, and as is noted in the opening sections of *Sacrosanctum Concilium*:

> To accomplish so great a work, Christ is always present in His Church, especially in her liturgical celebrations. He is present in the sacrifice of the Mass, not only in the person of His minister, "the same now offering, through the ministry of priests, who formerly offered himself on the cross," but especially under the Eucharistic species. By His power He is present in the sacraments, so that when a man baptizes it is really Christ Himself who baptizes. He is present in His word, since it is He Himself who speaks when the holy scriptures are read in the Church. He is pres-ent, lastly, when the Church prays and sings, for He promised: "Where

---

23. Robert Louis Wilken, *The Spirit of Christian Thought* (New Haven, CT: Yale University Press, 2003), 48.

24. See for example the numerous sermons of Gregory of Nazianzen on Christmas, Epiphany, and the Lord's Resurrection.

two or three are gathered together in my name, there am I in the midst of them" (Mt 18:20).

Christ indeed always associates the Church with Himself in this great work wherein God is perfectly glorified and men are sanctified. The Church is His beloved Bride who calls to her Lord, and through Him offers worship to the Eternal Father.

Rightly, then, the liturgy is considered as an exercise of the priestly office of Jesus Christ. In the liturgy the sanctification of the man is signified by signs perceptible to the senses, and is effected in a way which corresponds with each of these signs; in the liturgy the whole public worship is performed by the Mystical Body of Jesus Christ, that is, by the Head and His members.

From this it follows that every liturgical celebration, because it is an action of Christ the priest and of His Body which is the Church, is a sacred action surpassing all others; no other action of the Church can equal its efficacy by the same title and to the same degree.[25]

In 1963, the fathers of the Second Vatican Council clearly identified the liturgy as one of the primary areas of Church life that needed renewal. Most of their work involved continuing the work of the early pioneers of the Liturgical Movement, who saw the liturgy as having a deep pastoral impact on the community of faith. They identified the liturgy as a source or "fountain" from which everything else in the Church is poured forth, as is stated in *SC* 10:

From the liturgy, therefore, and especially from the Eucharist, as from a font, grace is poured forth upon us; and the sanctification of men in Christ and the glorification of God, to which all other activities of the Church are directed as toward their end, is achieved in the most efficacious possible way.

A similar sentiment is emphasized in *Ecclesia de Eucharistia*, where the late Pope John Paul II wrote:

The Church constantly draws her life from the redeeming sacrifice; she approaches it not only through faith-filled remembrance, but also through a real contact, since *this sacrifice is made present ever anew*, sacramentally perpetuated, in every community which offers it at the hands of the consecrated minister. The Eucharist thus applies to men and women

---

25. Second Vatican Council, Constitution on the Sacred Liturgy, *Sacrosanctum Concilium* (1963), 7.

today the reconciliation won once for all by Christ for mankind in every age. "The sacrifice of Christ and the sacrifice of the Eucharist are *one single sacrifice*." Saint John Chrysostom put it well: "We always offer the same Lamb, not one today and another tomorrow, but always the same one. For this reason the sacrifice is always only one. . . . even now we offer that victim who was once offered and who will never be consumed."[26]

Thus it is in the liturgy of the Church, especially the Eucharist, that we look to find the source and context for pastoral theology. It is in the liturgy that the local faith community gathers together to offer up their one prayer to the one Lord and receive the one bread and the one cup for the remission of sins and for life everlasting. It is also where the community is fed and nourished in order to go back to the world and to serve both God and neighbor. Ultimately, however, the liturgy is for the salvation of souls:

> There is no doubt that the essential success of pastoral care is achieved when souls are saved, when it succeeds in leading men in such a manner that at least in the hour of death they may find the right way and thus reach their goal. But it is a higher aim, and one more worthy of the Christian vocation, in fact, it is the true task of the Church, to lead the Christian people so that even here on earth they may come together in holy and joyous fellowship to glorify God, and to fulfill what St. Peter describes as the duty of God's people: "That you may declare His virtues, who has called you out of darkness into His marvelous light." (1 Pt 2:9). This is what exactly what the liturgy has attempted to do at all times.[27]

This statement was made by the liturgical theologian Josef Jungmann, one of the foremost liturgical scholars of this century. His comments are borrowed from an essay on the pastoral nature of the liturgy for a pre-Conciliar meeting at the Vatican in 1956. This meeting was convened in order to gather theologians from around the world to focus on the importance of a renewed interest in the pastoral nature of the liturgy. Their work eventually dovetailed into the work of the Second Vatican Council, especially *Sancrosanctum Concilium* and *Lumen Gentium*. Jungmann identified the purpose of the liturgy as

---

26. John Paul II, Encyclical Letter *Ecclesia De Eucharistia* (2003), 12. Quoting *Catechism of the Catholic Church*, 1367; In Epistolam ad Hebraeos Homiliae, Hom. 17, 3: PG 63, 131.

27. Josef Jungmann, *The Assisi Papers: Proceedings of the First International Congress of Pastoral Liturgy, Rome 1956* (Collegeville, MN: The Liturgical Press, 1957), 29.

"saving souls" and leading the flock to a deeper understanding and appreciation of their faith. The theologians at this meeting answered by looking to the liturgy as a source for renewal—not just rearranging the liturgical furniture or creating new prayer books, but looking to the liturgy as a source for theology and a path to a greater understanding of the Christian faith.

The Orthodox liturgical theologian Alexander Schmemann lived and studied in France during the time of the Liturgical Movement, and was greatly inspired by Catholic theologians. It was Schmemann who was the impetus of liturgical renewal in the East, especially in the Orthodox Church in North America.

Pastoral theology is indeed a large area of study, and the purpose of this chapter was to provide a small overview of the many theological issues and concerns regarding how pastoral theology is described. Additionally, the ever-widening gap between the academy and the parish creates other problems for pastoral theology. Schmemann was keenly aware of these problems, and attempted to put forth an answer by looking to the liturgy for possible solutions. Throughout his lifetime Schmemann looked to the sacramental life of the Church, especially the Eucharist, as a way to discuss our common life in Christ. It is here, in the liturgy, where we are able to identify Schmemann's sacramental vision of pastoral theology.

Chapter 2

Toward a Pastoral Renewal: Alexander Schmemann

Schmemann's writings are as important today as they were forty years ago. Many of the theological and spiritual issues against which Schmemann fought during his lifetime remain today, especially the problems of secularism and clericalism, as well as the misunderstanding of what pastoral ministry is. Many people read Schmemann for his focus on liturgy and miss his rich commentary on pastoral theology. Though Schmemann had a scholarly mind, he also had a pastoral awareness of the problems, trials, and tribulations that continually challenge the Church. This chapter will trace Schmemann's early theological and educational formation in France, locating his writings specifically within the milieu of the Liturgical Movement. Schmemann was deeply influenced by the great Roman Catholic liturgical theologians Louis Bouyer and Jean Daniélou, as well as Eastern Orthodox theologians Nicholas Afanasiev and Kyprian Kern. Afanasiev was one of the most important Orthodox theologians in post–World War II Paris, and his work and research deeply influenced the work of the Second Vatican Council, especially in the document *Lumen Gentium*. Kern was the mentor and teacher of both Schmemann and John Meyendorff, and his teaching can be seen in the writings of many of the Russian Parisian theologians, including Paul Evdokimov, of Lev Gillet, and Sergius Bulgakov.[1]

---

1. See Michael Plekon, *Living Icons: Persons of Faith in the Eastern Church* (South Bend, IN: University of Notre Dame Press, 2002) and Plekon, *Tradition Alive: On the Church and the Christian Life in Our Time* (New York: Rowman and Littlefield, 2003). See also Job Getcha, "From Master to Disciple: The Notion of 'Liturgical Theology' in Fr. Kiprian Kern and Fr. Alexander Schmemann," *St. Vladimir's Theological Quarterly* 53, no. 2–3 (2009): 251–272.

Schmemann's most important contribution to theology is his emphasis on the centrality of worship in the life and practice of the Church. His writings reflect his passion for liturgical worship not only as an academic subject for study and reflection, but as the formative factor for theological inquiry; according to Schmemann, the Scriptures, doctrine, faith, practices, and prayers of the Church are expressed and fully realized in liturgy—specifically, in the Eucharist. In his essay "Liturgical Theology, Theology of Liturgy, and Liturgical Reform," Schmemann presents us with his vision of liturgical theology:

> But then liturgical theology—and I cannot overemphasize this—is not that part of theology, that "discipline," which deals with liturgy "in itself," has liturgy as its specific "object," but first of all and above everything else, the attempt to grasp the "theology" as revealed in and through liturgy.[2]

During his tenure as dean, Schmemann flourished as a scholar, teacher, preacher, pastor, and theologian. In addition to his administrative position at the seminary, Schmemann traveled throughout the United States and Canada, presenting papers at numerous colleges and universities. He also served as an adjunct professor at both Union and General Theological Seminaries, as well as at Columbia University.[3] His work was also known outside theological circles, and he received honorary doctorates from Butler University, Lafayette College, and Iona College. During this time in his career, Schmemann devoted his efforts to writing articles and books, as well as recording weekly sermons in Russian for Radio Liberty, which broadcasted them in the Soviet Union during the Cold War period.

Despite all the progress that Schmemann made as dean of St. Vladimir's Orthodox Theological Seminary Crestwood, New York, he found the liturgical life of the Russian Orthodox Church (Metropolia)[4] in disarray. For instance, services were generally conducted in Old Church Slavonic, an ancient form of the Russian language, which few people understood. Furthermore, greater emphasis was placed on "private" services, such as memorial services for the

---

2. Thomas Fisch, editor, *Liturgy and Traditions: Theological Reflections of Alexander Schmemann* (Crestwood, NY: St. Vladimir's Seminary Press, 1990), 39.

3. John Meyendorff, "Protopresbyter Alexander Schmemann: A Life Worth Living," *St. Vladimir's Theological Quarterly* 28, no. 1 (1984): 4.

4. The Russian Orthodox Church in North America later became the Orthodox Church of America.

departed and private thanksgiving services called *moliebens*. Likewise, the majority of people received Holy Communion infrequently, either on Christmas or during Holy Week and Easter. Additionally, very few parishes had a full liturgical cycle that included the prescribed feast days and Holy Days around Christmas and Easter. Children attended weekly Russian school rather than Sunday school, and there were few published books for adult education, except for the popular Orthodox catechism, *Zakon Bozhi*, also known by its English translation as *God's Law*.[5] Parishioners were expected merely to fulfill their sacramental obligation, attending Confession and Communion once per year, as well as their financial obligation to the parish, in order to be considered members in good standing.[6]

Schmemann was exposed to many other administrative, ethnic, and jurisdictional problems that plagued the young Orthodox Church in America. However, in the midst of this seemingly chaotic situation, he managed to disseminate his liturgical and Eucharistic vision of the Church. He influenced a generation of priests and laity, and brought a much-needed Eucharistic revival to the Church.

Schmemann's work in North America included acting as the theological advisor to the Holy Synod of Bishops, the highest administrative position in the Orthodox Church in America. This position allowed Schmemann to have a hand in greater reforms and renewal on a national level; his Eucharistic vision and emphasis on the liturgy influenced not only the bishops, but all levels of Church life. Schmemann helped to bring about liturgical renewal in the parishes through English language services, as well as frequent Confession and Communion for the laity, just in his own lifetime. In a 1972 report to the Holy Synod entitled "Confession and Communion," Schmemann wrote:

---

5. Ibid.

6. For a thorough analysis of the general liturgical life in the Orthodox Church in North America in the mid-20th century, see the recent work from Paul Meyendorff especially, "Fr. Alexander Schmemann's Liturgical Legacy in America," *St. Vladimir's Theological Quarterly* 53, no. 2–3 (2009): 319–330; "The Liturgical Path of Orthodoxy in America," *St. Vladimir's Theological Quarterly* 40, no. 1 (1996): 43–64; and "Liturgical Life in the Parish: Present and Future Realities," in Anton C. Vrame, ed., *The Orthodox Parish in America: Faithfulness to the Past and Responsibility for the Future* (Brookline, MA: Holy Cross Orthodox Press, 2003), 143–254.

If I began this report on the sacraments with general considerations concerning the situation in the world as well as in the Church it is because of
my deep conviction that the new interest in sacramental practice and
discipline stems from this very crisis and is directly related to it. I am convinced that the question of lay participation in the Divine Mysteries is
indeed the key question of our entire Church life; it is upon the solution
of this question that the future of our Church, her renewal or her decay,
ultimately depends.[7]

This statement reflects Schmemann's constant struggle against reducing the Church to mere rules or rituals with clergy-only participation,
drawing out instead the reality of the Church as a worshipping
community. In this passage, as elsewhere, Schmemann focuses
attention on the Eucharistic liturgy as the source and true nature of
the Church.

Schmemann railed against reductionism in Church life—
notably, the common early 20th century belief among Orthodox and
Catholics that the liturgy was primarily for the clergy. People thought
that the laity had no role except to be present for the services, that
liturgy was a ritual performed in a different language that contained
the awe and mystery of the divine. Schmemann's emphasis on the
Eucharistic liturgy as the *raison d'être* of the Church was his answer to
these various reductions, which became the lens through which he
viewed the relationship between the clergy and the laity in the Church.

It is in the area of liturgical theology that Schmemann made
the greatest contribution to Orthodox theology. However, while
always a scholar and theologian, Schmemann managed to convey his
vision of the Church not only to academicians, but to the entire
Church. He often bemoaned the fact that too many theologians spoke
and wrote for the pulpit rather than for the pew.[8] He saw this as a
disservice to theology, since the primary goal or aim of theology is the
sanctification of the whole Church, not just the clergy or academics.
Schmemann's vision of the Church as the Body of Christ, fed and
nourished on the Eucharist and alive and very much in this world,
was a message that he carried not only to the Holy Synod of Bishops

---

7. Alexander Schmemann, *Confession and Communion Report to the Holy Synod of Bishops of the
Orthodox Church in America* (Syosset, NY: Orthodox Church in America, 1972).

8. Schmemann, *Journals*, 93, 229.

but to all levels of Orthodox Church life. He especially carried it to the parish.

Schmemann brought this Eucharistic vision to dioceses, deaneries, and parishes throughout North America. His impact on parochial life can be seen today in the annual Liturgical Institutes hosted on the campus of St. Vladimir's Seminary, where clergy and laity join together for a week of prayer, theological inquiry, and fellowship. The Institutes were patterned after the Liturgical Weeks at St. Serge Theological Academy, which were started by Frs. Kern and Afanasiev as a way to bring together Orthodox, Catholic, Anglican, and Lutheran scholars and clergy leaders for a week of study, prayer, and reflection on liturgy and worship.[9]

Other important pastoral contributions include Schmemann's brief but informative introductions to prayer books and booklets for the feast days throughout the year, his numerous articles on Church life that were published in *The Orthodox Church* newspaper, the many public talks and retreats that he delivered across the United States and Canada, and of course his pastoral influence at St. Vladimir's Seminary. However, it was his teaching on the Eucharist that had the most impact on the Orthodox Church in the last century. In his funeral sermon for Schmemann, Metropolitan Theodosius, the former primate of the Orthodox Church in America, stated:

> So much of what we now take for granted in our Church's spiritual and liturgical life has been implanted, cultivated and nourished by Fr. Alexander's teaching. In season and out of season, he was an eloquent and tireless witness to the living Orthodox tradition. At the heart of his approach to theology was the insight which sees the living connection between the worship of the Church and the Christian faith. This insight enabled Fr. Alexander literally to open our eyes to the Eucharist, to what the Divine Liturgy is and what it says and what it means.[10]

---

9. In a short report from the fourth annual Liturgical Week in Paris Schmemann mentions the diversity of participants. Catholics included Dom Bernard Botte, OSB, from Mont César, Belgium; Dom J. Capelle, OSB; Dom Burkhard Neunheuser, OSB, from Maria Laach; Rev. Balthasar Ficher of Trier; Rev. Alponse Raes, SJ; and Dom Olivier Rousseau from Chevetogne. Protestants included Rev. Allan MacArthur from Glasgow; Rev. E.C. Varah, London, from the Church of England; and Prof. Harold Riesenfeld from Uppsala, Sweden. Orthodox included Prof. Andre Grabar of the College de France; Bishop Cassian; Prof. T. Spasky; and Schmemann himself. See Schmemann "The Fourth Liturgical Week at St. Serigus in Paris," accessed online http://www.schmemann.org/byhim/liturgicalweek.html.

10. *St. Vladimir's Theological Quarterly* 28 (1984): 33.

For nearly four decades, Schmemann was spiritual father, pastor, and priest to hundreds of seminarians. Many of his former students later became bishops, priests, deacons, professors, and lay leaders in the Church. These accomplishments reveal a man who was very much a scholar and theologian, yet at the same time always a pastor to his flock, whether he was hearing confessions of seminary students, presenting talks to an ecumenical gathering, or preaching a sermon on Sunday morning. Schmemann's emphasis on the pastoral nature of the liturgy, which is implicit in his writings, will be made explicit in this book.

Alexander Schmemann and Liturgical Theology

Before entering into a discussion of Schmemann's liturgical theology, it is important to locate his thought within a historical and theological context. Schmemann's writings inspired a liturgical renewal and revival in North America, but his historical and theological roots were planted in European soil during the height of the Liturgical Movement. Thus it is his immediate theological background that provides us with a larger picture of his vision of liturgy, the Eucharist, and pastoral theology.

The Early Years

Alexander Schmemann was born on September 13, 1921, in Tallin, Estonia, to Dmitri Schmemann and Anna Shishkova. Dmitri and Anna had twin boys whom they named Andre and Alexander. They bore a daughter, Elena, in 1919, but she died on Christmas Eve in 1925 from diphtheria and scarlet fever.[11] The Schmemanns moved to Belgrade for a little over a year, then relocated to Paris in order to look for work and for a better life for their family. Life was very difficult at that time. In Paris, the Schmemann family joined the growing Russian émigré community, comprised of Russians with various intellectual and social backgrounds including artists, writers, politicians, and theologians, many of whom left Russia on the eve of the 1917–1918 Russian Revolution and expected to return to their

---

11. Juliana Schmemann, *My Journey with Father Alexander* (Montreal: Alexander Press, 2007), 14.

homeland after the upheaval had ended. However, for most of these emigrants, this dream would never be realized.[12] First the rise of the Soviet Bolshevik government, then the Russian Civil War hampered travel back to Russia. Most of those who had left remained in the West.

Life in the West was not very easy. Meyendorff, Schmemann's longtime friend, colleague, and confidant, once remarked that the Russian émigrés lived in social, cultural, and religious isolation from everyone else. Their extreme poverty, together with their Orthodox faith and Russian heritage, prohibited them from assimilating fully into their new Western European milieu.[13] It was in this Western culture that both Meyendorff and Schmemann lived and studied, together with a host of other Russian émigrés who had left their former homeland to make a new beginning in the West.[14]

Some émigrés found safe haven in Central European cities such as Belgrade, Berlin, and Prague, as well as in Western European cities such as London and Paris. Wherever they went, these Russian emigrants established close-knit religious communities and created their own social and cultural activities. The Church became the focus of both religious life and social experience, and was thereby central to Schmemann's life.[15]

Worship was important for the Schmemann family. Together with Andrei and his parents, Alexander attended the St. Alexander Nevsky Cathedral on *rue Daru* in Paris, where he became an altar server and later a sub-deacon.[16] St. Nevsky Cathedral was the Episcopal See of Metropolitan Evlogy (Georgievsky) of Volhynia, the acting Metropolitan of the Russian Orthodox Exarchate in Western Europe. Evlogy was a strong pastor and leader who participated in numerous ecumenical and theological discussions and conferences

---

12. Sophie Koulumzine, *Many Worlds: A Russian Life* (Crestwood, NY: St. Vladimir's Seminary Press, 1980). See also Marc Raeff, *Russian Abroad: A Cultural History of the Russian Emigration 1919–1939* (Oxford, Oxford University Press, 1990); Catherine Andreyev, *Russia Abroad: Prague and the Russian Diaspora 1918-1938* (New Haven, CT: Yale University Press, 2004).

13. Meyendorff, "A Life Worth Living," 146. See also Helene Iswolsky, *No Time to Grieve: An Autobiographical Journey,* (NY: Hippocrene Books, 1986) and Paul Anderson, *No East or West* (NY: YMCA Press, 1988).

14. Juliana Schmemann points out the strong anti-Russian fervor in France during World War II and the period thereafter in, see *My Journey with Father Alexander*, 43.

15. Schmemann, *Journals*, 293.

16. Ibid., 146.

across Europe, and helped to establish the St. Serge Theological Academy in Paris. St. Serge was founded in 1925 as a Russian Orthodox theological academy on equal footing with the famous theological academies in St. Petersburg, Moscow, Kazan, and Kiev. [17] St. Serge was the home not only to Russian-born immigrants, but also to local French Orthodox students, as well as those from Greece and the Middle East. Even today, St. Serge maintains an ethnically diverse student body. [18]

Schmemann began his studies at the famous Lycée Carnot in Versailles, a military academy for boys. Later he was transferred to an upper level *gymnasium,* the European equivalent of high school, where he enjoyed a classical education of literature, music, art, and culture. In his later journals he often commented on his early childhood love for culture, reflecting on the influence that General Rimsky-Korsakov and Professor Weidle had on him. [19] His love for art, poetry, and music would continue throughout his adult years, as he himself notes throughout his journals. [20] Schmemann was interested in politics, modern society, and culture, and was well-versed in both Russian and French literature.

Schmemann enrolled at the University of Paris and then matriculated at the St. Serge Theological Institute, where he received his theological training and education. St. Serge was a premier school for theology in Western Europe, and was home to noteworthy professors and theologians such as the famous priests Sergius Bulgakov,

---

17. Evlogy was himself a man of extraordinary energy. In addition to his regular episcopal duties, he hosted numerous theological conferences and was the spiritual father to many clergy and laity, especially Mother Maria Skobtsova, Sister Joanna Reitlinger, Fr. Dmitiri Kleppinin, and Archimandrite Kyprian Kern—all of whom were active in the Russian religious renaissance in France. Evlogy was also very active in the ecumenical movement in Europe. For more information about the establishment of the St. Sergius Theological Academy and Metropolitan Evlogy see Donald Lowrie, *Saint Sergius in Paris: The Orthodox Theological Institute* (England: Society for Promoting Christian Knowledge, 1954).

18. For more information about St. Serge Orthodox Theological Institute, visit their website at www.saint-serge.net.

19 Professor Vladimir Wiedle was an expert in philosophy and art, and was very influential upon the young Schmemann. Wiedle eventually emigrated to the United States, where he became reacquainted with the Schmemann family.

20. Even though Schmemann was a dean, frequent guest speaker and lecturer, priest, confessor, husband, and father, he managed to read widely and deeply, especially biographies, philosophy, poetry, and short stories. See for example Schmemann, *Journals,* 2, 3, 17, 18, 31, 101, 138, 215, 235, 305.

Kern, and Afanasiev, as well as the lay theologians A. V. Kartashev, and V. V. Zenkovsky. Kartashev was one of the major figures in the 1917–1918 All Russian Council held in Moscow, and, as lay leader, he was partly responsible for the agenda of this council, which was supposed to make important changes in the Church for the renewal of worship, including the translation of texts from Old Church Slavonic into Russian, and exploring the possibility of reinstating the female diaconate.[21]

While at St. Serge, Schmemann received the equivalent of a Master of Divinity degree. He then became a lecturer in Church history, following in the footsteps of his mentor, Kartashev. Meyendorff commented that Schmemann's first love was ecclesiastical history, and notes that Schmemann had planned to write a doctoral dissertation on Byzantine theocracy, only to put history aside in order to study liturgy.[22] However, Schmemann never abandoned his historical studies, and rooted his liturgical writings in a historical context. Schmemann also reflected on the historical development of the Church in his many articles, books, sermons, and talks.

During his time at St. Serge, Schmemann met Juliana Ossorgine, who was studying classics at the Sorbonne. Juliana, like Alexander, was from a Russian émigré family who found their home in Paris and then moved to nearby Clamart.[23] Alexander and Juliana were married on January 31, 1943, at the Alexander Nevsky Cathedral on *rue Daru*. After their wedding, the Schmemanns lived in Clamart, then relocated to l'Etang-la-Ville, a western suburb of Paris, where they lived a very austere life.[24] The war in Europe took its toll on many people, including the hundreds—if not thousands—of immigrants

---

21. See Alexander A. Bogolepov *Church Reforms in Russia 1905–1918: A Commemoration of the All Russian Church Council of 1917–1918* (Bridgeport, CT: Publication Committee of the Metropolitan Council of the Russian Orthodox Church in America, 1966); Nicolas Zernov *The Russian Religious Renaissance of the Twentieth Century* (New York: Harper and Row, 1963); and Hyacinthe Destivelle *Le concile de Moscou (1917–1918): La création des institutions conciliaires de l'Eglise orthodoxe russe* (Paris: Edition du Cerf, 2006).

22. Meyendorff, "A Life Worth Living," 147.

23. Juliana and her family were members of the famous Ossorgine family, who were related to the Romanov Dynasty which even boasted of an Orthodox saint, St. Juliana Lazerenko, who lived in Medieval Russia between 1530–1603. For more information about the Ossorgine and Schmemann families, see Serge Schmemann, *Echoes of a Native Land: Two Centuries of a Russian Village* (New York: Vintage Books, 1997).

24. According to Juliana, their living quarters were very austere: "It was a wooden shack, an outside toilet, one faucet of cold water, a primitive wood burning stove that was always smoking." Juliana Schmemann, *My Journey with Father Alexander,* 44.

who had few job opportunities. Life was extremely difficult for the Schmemanns, as for most people. Juliana recounts many nights that they had to stay in bomb shelters because of the constant shelling or fear of attacks. In order to supplement their meager income, both Juliana and Alexander took on additional work. They were invited to serve as Russian translators at a business school called *Hautes Etudes Commerciales*. Later both Juliana and Alexander got work as Russian-French translators for La Pasionaria, the general conference of the Spanish Communist Party that was meeting in Paris.[25] The extra income allowed them to purchase clothes for their children and extra food for the family.

Schmemann was ordained to the diaconate on November 4, 1946, and to the priesthood on November 30, 1946, by Archbishop Vladimir (Tikhonistsky) and was assigned to help Fr. Kern with Sts. Constantine and Helen parish in Clamart, just southwest of Paris.[26] By this time the young Schmemann was well on his way to a teaching career, often assisting Professor Kartashev in his Church history classes.

Schmemann's Theological Formation

Schmemann lived, studied, and worshipped in a theologically diverse and free-thinking religious and social community. From the early 1920s to the end of the 1950s, the Orthodox community in Paris was reveling in a theological renaissance. For lack of a better term, some scholars, such as Paul Valliere and others, have referred to this major theological movement and the resultant body of literature as the "Russian School" or "Paris School."[27] The Paris School was not

---

25. Juliana Schmemann, *My Journey with Father Alexander*, 44.

26. Nicholas Berdiaev, one of the major philosophers and thinkers in the Russian religious renaissance in Paris, also lived in Clamart. Every Sunday evening he held open salons where people would come to discuss politics, art, culture, music, theology, and philosophy.

27. Of the Paris School, Church historian Antoine Arjakovsky has said, "The School of Paris is a reality difficult to identify. It cannot be conceptualized. I would say that it is a movement, a symbolic reality, which the French historian Pierre Nora calls a 'place of memory,' that is, a certain relation to the Tradition of the Church . . . And then again the collective memory of the Paris school is not very precise. Nobody really knows when it starts and when it finishes!" Arjakovsky, "The Paris School and Eucharistic Ecclesiology in the 20th Century" (unpublished paper, St. Vladimir's Seminary, Crestwood, NY, 2004). See also Bishop Hilarion Alfeyev, "Theology on the Threshold of the Twentieth Century" (paper presented at the international scholarly conference "The Russian Orthodox Church from 1943 to the present," Transfiguration Monastery, Bose, Italy, September 15–17, 1999); Paul Valliere, *Modern Russian Theology:*

a thoroughly organized movement, but an informal gathering of like-minded people who were interested in a theological renewal and revival in the Church. Although this was not a single, identifiable school of thought, these theologians' writings on the nature of the Church and the role of the Eucharist, as well as the liturgical renaissance which was taking place in both the Eastern and Western Churches, provided fertile soil for reflecting on theology, ecclesiology, liturgy, and the Church fathers. This Russian religious renaissance was essential to Schmemann's formation. While Schmemann does not specifically mention other liturgical reformers that influenced him, it is quite apparent from reading his books and articles that he appreciated the work of Catholic theologians including Gregory Dix, osb, Jean Daniélou, sj, and Bernard Botte, osb. It is difficult to discern exactly how he was inspired, but almost every page of his writings bears a glimpse of either his teachers or the liturgical theologians who were popular through his formative years.[28]

Scholars like Afanasiev, Schmemann, Meyendorff, Kern, Bulgakov, Kartashev, Gillet, Evdokimov, and Mother Maria Skobtsova, were the lifeblood of this Russian émigré theological renaissance. In his book *Living Icons*, Plekon notes the complex relationships that these persons enjoyed:

> Paul Evdokimov was among Father Bulgakov's students in the first class to graduate from St. Serge Theological Institute. Father Lev (Gillet) attended Bulgakov's classes, though he was not formally enrolled. Mother Maria was a spiritual child of his, and Father Afanasieff also studied under and later taught with Father Bulgakov. Afanasieff, in turn, was a close friend and colleague of Evdokimov and the teacher of Father Schmemann, directing the later into his own "Eucharistic ecclesiology." Schmemann later would craft a distinctive approach that he called "liturgical theology."[29]

Bukharev, Soloviev, Bulgakov: Orthodox Theology in a New Key (Grand Rapids, MI: William Eerdmans, 2000). The term "Russian School" was coined by Alexander Schmemann when he referred to the Russian theological renaissance in the West, especially in his bibliographic essay. Valliere uses the term "Russian School" in reference to the same theological trend.

28. Throughout his journals, Schmemann often reflected on the persons and personalities that inspired him, many of whom were active in the Paris School, notably his mentor, Kyprian Kern.

29. Plekon, *Living Icons*, 17 (parenthesis mine).

One could also add the long-time friendship between Schmemann and Meyendorff. Though Meyendorff was a few years his junior, they both studied at St. Serge, and Meyendorff followed Schmemann to the United States, where they were colleagues until Schmemann's untimely death in 1983. Meyendorff and Afanasiev were the examiners for Schmemann's doctoral research on liturgical theology.[30] After Schmemann's death, Meyendorff was named dean of St. Vladimir's Seminary.

Georges Florovsky, the noteworthy Patristic scholar and Orthodox theologian, also had a significant impact on Schmemann's vision of theology. While in Paris, Florovsky taught Church history and patristics, developing what was later called the neo-patristic synthesis, which looked back to the Fathers as a way toward a theological renewal.[31] Florovsky left St. Serge to be the new dean of St. Vladimir's Orthodox Theological Seminary in New York, then left St. Vladimir's to teach at both Harvard and Princeton Universities. While Schmemann didn't devote his work entirely to Church history, he often commented how a thorough knowledge and understanding of history is essential to understanding the meaning and the message of the liturgy.

This small community of like-minded persons reveals a genuine sense of reflection, investigation, and renewal in the Russian émigré community during this theological flowering in Paris. Not all the scholars of the Paris School were considered close friends, but they all were actively seeking the rich theological and liturgical tradition of the ancient Church that had been lost for many centuries. They attempted to return to the sources—namely the Scriptures, patristics, and the liturgy—in order to uncover the richness of theology.

For many of these Orthodox theologians, the relationship between liturgy and Church became the primary subject for thought

---

30. Meyendorff and Schmemann were very close, working side by side at St. Vladimir's Seminary, giving lectures, speaking to ecumenical groups, and building up the Orthodox Church in America. Meyendorff died on July 22, 1992, after complications from pancreatic cancer. For more background on Fr. Meyendorff see Bradley Nassif, ed., *New Perspectives in Historical Theology: Essays in Honor of John Meyendorff* (Grand Rapids, MI: Eerdmans, 1996).

31. See Andrew Blane, ed., *Georges Florovsky: Russian Intellectual, Orthodox Churchman* (Crestwood, NY: St. Vladimir's Seminary Press, 1993). Schmemann and Florovsky were among the Russian Orthodox delegates to the inaugural conference of the World Council of Churches held in Amsterdam in 1948.

and reflection. Afanasiev, Bulgakov, and Kern focused on the interrelationship of Church, liturgy, ecclesiology, and Eucharist, as well as the relationships between clergy and laity—an important topic in Roman Catholic circles as well. These thinkers influenced Schmemann's own understanding of the Church as a community gathered together for the Eucharistic celebration, fed and nourished on the Word of God, and then sent out into the world for mission and evangelism. Schmemann would later develop his own thoughts about the nature of the Eucharist, which are apparent throughout his writings, especially his magnum opus, *The Eucharist*.

Nicholas Afanasiev was an inspiration to the young Schmemann. He was a pioneer of what was later called Eucharistic ecclesiology: in almost every page of his writings, one can see the centrality of the Eucharist as a source of both theology and reflection on the Church. His major works, *The Church of the Holy Spirit*, *The Lord's Supper*, and *The Limits of the Church*, were important contributions to Eastern theology at that time. [32] After reading through the major patristic authors, Afanasiev deeply saw that the early vision of the Church was more than an institution of clergy who performed the sacraments to benefit a passive laity. Rather, it was the living and organic Body of Christ, comprised of both clergy and laity, joined around the one altar in order to celebrate the Eucharist:

> Participation in "the mystery of the gathering" manifests both the life of the Church and our life in the Church. The Eucharist is the center towards which everything aims and in which everything meets. The Body of Christ is realized only in the Eucharist: "This is my body." Where the Body is, there Christ is. Also, on the other hand; where Christ is, there His Body is. The advent of Christ in the Eucharist is accomplished by the Spirit. The Eucharist is not only a gathering, but it is also the very Supper of our Lord . . . "when you gather in the Church . . ." The Eucharist is the gathering of the people of God in Christ, and this gathering includes

---

32. Nicholas Afanasiev, *The Church of The Holy Spirit*, ed. Michael Plekon, trans. Vitaly Permiakov (South Bend, IN: The University of Notre Dame Press, 2007). See also Afanasiev, "The Church Which Presides in Love" in *The Primacy of Peter: Essays in Ecclesiology and the Early Church*, ed. John Meyendorff (Crestwood, NY: St. Vladimir's Seminary Press, 1992); Aidan Nichols, *Theology in the Russian Diaspora: Church, Fathers, Eucharist in Nikolai Afanasiev 1883–1966* (Cambridge: Cambridge University Press, 1989); Plekon, *Living Icons: Persons of Faith in the Eastern Church* (South Bend, IN: The University of Notre Dame Press, 2003) 149–176. Alvian Smirensky (Translator), "Lord's Supper," in Nicholas Afanasiev, *Limits of the Church*, Vitaly Permiakov (Translator). Unpublished Manuscript.

within itself the idea of concelebration. The people of God gather
together in the Church for the worship offered unto God. Each person
serves (i.e., concelebration) together with all the others under the presi-
dency of one. There is no gathering in Church without concelebration and
there is no concelebration apart from the gathering. There is no "Lord's
Supper" without the participants and there are no participants apart from
him who presides. [33]

According to Afanasiev, the Church is truly the Body of Christ when
it gathers together for the Eucharist. He coined the term Eucharistic
ecclesiology to define this theological understanding of the Eucharistic
nature of the Church. [34] In other words, he underscored the image of a
Church that is established in the local Eucharistic gathering—without
reducing the Church to isolated Eucharistic communities as separate
entities; on the contrary, he emphasized that the fullness of the
Church is present at each and every Eucharistic gathering.

Another important aspect of Afanasiev's writing was his
encouragement to the faithful of frequent reception of Holy
Communion. This was a common theme across the Liturgical
Movement, for most Christians had a strong sense of the juridical
nature of the Church, believing that the most important thing was
the institution of the Church, and did not see the Eucharist as the
central symbol and sign of the unity of the Church.

Afanasiev's writings were deeply pastoral, in that he encouraged active participation by the entire Body of Christ, clergy and laity
alike, and was a proponent of frequent Communion during a time
when very few people received the Eucharist. To this end, he emphasized the importance of concelebration in the liturgy, explaining that
true concelebration is not comprised only of clergy standing around
the altar, but of clergy and laity gathered together at the one altar,
offering the one prayer of praise to God, and receiving the one
Eucharist and Chalice for the salvation of the world. This concelebration of the entire people of God reveals the unity and harmony of the
Church. Afanasiev taught carefully, as Schmemann later would,
that the Eucharist should not be understood merely in terms of rubrics

---

33. Afanasiev, *Church of the Holy Spirit*, 2.

34. The Eucharistic nature of the Church was not entirely new with Afanasiev, but can be
seen in the early patristic witness, especially the letters of St. Ignatius of Antioch.

or ritual, but of the worshipping community becoming the Body of Christ.

Afanasiev's work was also very influential in the Roman Catholic Church, especially in the proceedings of the Second Vatican Council. Afanasiev was the only Orthodox theologian who was mentioned by name in the working session of the Council that produced the Constitution on the Church, *Lumen Gentium*.[35] However, Afanasiev was not without his detractors.[36] Both Catholic and Orthodox scholars have questioned Afanasiev's emphasis on the local Eucharistic gathering, seeing in it a diminishment of the universality of the Eucharist in terms of the larger Church.[37] Nevertheless, Schmemann's thoughts on the Eucharist were heavily influenced by those of Afanasiev, who was instrumental in his theological training and formation.

Another very important person in the life of the young Schmemann was Archimandrite Kyprian Kern. Kern taught patristics, Church history, and liturgics at St. Serge. Originally trained as a lawyer, Kern later turned his attention to the study of theology, writing his doctoral dissertation on the mystical theology of Gregory Palamas. Kern lived in Belgrade for a while before emigrating to Paris, where he accepted a teaching post. In addition to his teaching position at St. Serge, Kern served as the chaplain for one of Mother Maria Skobtsova's houses of hospitality on *rue Lourmel* in Paris. Due to personality conflicts he left *rue Lourmel* for Sts. Constantine and Helen parish in Clamart, where the young Schmemann served as his assistant for some time.[38]

---

35. Plekon, *Living Icons*, 150.

36. Ibid., 29.

37. Ibid., 30.

38. Kern is perhaps one of the lesser known persons in the Paris School. He was tonsured a monk by the famous Metropolitan Anthony Khrapovitsky and then ordained a priest. He taught at the Bitola Seminary in Serbia for a short while before emigrating to Paris, where Fr. Bulgakov invited him to teach patristics and liturgics. While not a prolific author, he nonetheless wrote several books and articles that were influential to the pastoral understanding of liturgy. For more information, see Kern, *Orthodox Pastoral Service*, ed. William C. Mills, trans. Mary Goddard, (Rollinsford, NH: Orthodox Research Institute, 2009); Archimandrite Kyprian Kern, "Two Models of the Pastorate: Levitical and Prophetic" in Michael Plekon, ed., *Tradition Alive*, 107–120; Khrapovitsky, "Reminiscences of Metropolitan Anthony Khrapovitsky, Part I," trans. Alexander Lisenko, *Divine Ascent: A Journal of the Orthodox Faith* 9 (2004) 107–162; Khrapovitsky, "Reminiscences of Anthony Khrapovitsky, Part II," trans. Alexander Lisenko *Divine Ascent: A Journal of the Orthodox Faith* 10 (2005) 50–87.

One of Kern's major works is a reflection on the Eucharistic liturgy, simply titled *Eucharist*. Kern made such an impression on the young Schmemann that he dedicated his doctoral dissertation to Kern.[39] Schmemann's wife Juliana recalled Kern's influence on the young Schmemann, "He (Kern) did not have any new ideas. He was not the one who, say, pushed us into more frequent communion. But he preached that emphasis on the Eucharist as being central and being beautiful."[40] Meyendorff notes that the conservatism of the Eastern Church at the time prevented Kern from going further with liturgical reforms: "The reading of the anaphora aloud was something which Kyprian strongly preached, he was saying this should be the norm. But he himself would not dare do it. This conservative frozenness of the whole thing, the Tradition (with a small 't') was still very strong."[41] Kern also emphasized the pastoral nature of the liturgy—especially the Eucharistic liturgy—in his writings, most notably his magnum opus, *Orthodox Pastoral Service*. In this book Kern outlines his understanding of pastoral theology and the liturgy. He envisions the Eucharist as the source for the understanding and practice of pastoral care in the Church:

> The priest first and foremost is a liturgist, one who loves the liturgy. Priesthood consists mainly of liturgy: The Eucharist and the mystical union with Christ in the mystery of the body and the blood. This is the unity of the pastor and his flock. The spiritual life of the priest, first and foremost, must be experienced in his own life as well in the life of his flock. The Eucharistic Church should, above all, envelope the priest. It is impossible for the Eucharist to exist outside the Church and for the Church to exist without the Eucharist. The Church fathers did not write treatises about the Church, but lived in her and by her; neither did they write in the classical theological scholastic period treatises about the Holy Spirit, but lived in the Spirit.[42]

Kern demonstrates throughout the work how intimately the priest is connected to his flock through the Eucharistic celebration, and also

---

39. Archimandrite Kyprian Kern, *Eucharistia* (Paris: YMCA Press, 1947).

40. Elena Silk, "The Eucharistic Revival Movement in the Orthodox Church in America: Past, Present, and Future" (M.Div. thesis, St. Vladimir's Orthodox Theological Seminary, 1986), 25.

41. Ibid., 28.

42. Kern, *Orthodox Pastoral Service*, 57–58.

how the priest must always be a lover of the liturgy, not necessarily in the liturgical minutiae or rubrics, but in the overall sense of worship. Kern argued that it is through worship that people encounter the Gospel of repentance and are lead to a renewed faith in the crucified Christ, from which they are sent out to serve their neighbor. Kern also wrote adamantly against the abuse of clerical authority: The Church was given to the entire people of God as the Body of Christ, and while there might be official offices and ministries within this body, there is no room for the abuse of power.[43]

A final influence upon Schmemann's love for the liturgy was Sergius Bulgakov, a formidable author and theologian who linked ecclesiology with the Eucharistic liturgy.[44] Bulgakov's own life and legacy is actually quite extraordinary. Born into a clergy family in Livny, in the Oryol province, he grew up in the Russian Orthodox Church. He entered the local seminary, but had a theological crisis and had to leave. Two years after leaving Oryol, he enrolled at the Lycée à Yelets where he studied law, economics, literature, and philosophy.

In his youth, Bulgakov was a Marxist and an atheist, focusing his attention on social dynamics and history, but in midlife he returned to the Orthodox Church of his childhood with great fervor. Bulgakov attended the famous 1917–1918 Moscow All Russian Council. Soon after, he was ordained to the priesthood by Bishop Feodor of Volokolam on July 24, 1918. Bulgakov later went on to serve as professor of theology, author, speaker, and ecumenist. His writing reflects a deep love for the Church and for the unity of Christians everywhere. In a brief autobiographical essay titled "Hagia Sophia," Bulgakov reflects on the sheer beauty and importance of that famous Cathedral in Istanbul dedicated to the Holy Spirit. While visiting this grand cathedral, he realized that it showed the unity not

---

43. See Kern, "Two Models of the Pastorates," in Plekon, *Tradition Alive, 109–120.*

44. Plekon, *Living Icons,* 48. See also the many new translations of Bulgakov's work by Boris Jakim: *Bride of the Lamb* (Grand Rapids, MI: Eerdmans, 2002); *Lamb of God* (Grand Rapids, MI: Eerdmans, 2007); *The Comforter* (Grand Rapids, MI: Eerdmans, 2004); *Friend of the Bridegroom: On the Orthodox Veneration of the Forerunner* (Grand Rapids, MI: Eerdmans, 2003); *Social Teaching in Modern Russian Orthodox Theology.* (New Haven, CT: The Variable Press, 1995); and *Apocatastasis and Transfiguration.* (New Haven, CT: The Variable Press, 1995). See also Sergei Bulgakov, *Sophia, the Wisdom of God: A Brief Summary of Sophiology,* trans. Patrick Thompson, O. Fielding Clark, and Xenia Brakevich (New York: Paisley Press, Inc., 1937).

only between heaven and earth but of all Christians everywhere, since it was the central place of worship for the entire Byzantine Empire. Bulgakov kept this theme of the unity of Christians with him wherever he traveled, and he devoted his preaching, teaching, and pastoral care to living out this common calling of unity and love for humanity, and all creation. Bulgakov ultimately saw this unity take shape in the Eucharistic liturgy. In the liturgy all of creation is represented: the entire cosmos, the living and the dead, the clergy and the laity, all gathered around the one altar offering thanksgiving to God. It is this gathering in a bond of love that becomes the foundation for ecclesiastical ministry.

Bulgakov had many disciples and followers, one of whom was the young Schmemann. Alexander and Juliana attended the weekly Divine Liturgy every Thursday morning in a small chapel where Bulgakov presided. Toward the end of Bulgakov's life, when he was dying of throat cancer, he continued to celebrate this weekly Liturgy with only a handful of people in attendance. Juliana comments on these early liturgies: "he was wearing very, very light weight vestments and it was really an angelic sight. This man without a voice, who was the liturgy. I think that maybe this is when both of us—we communed in the liturgy the most."[45]

It is this image of Bulgakov as a priest, a man of prayer, and a celebrant of the liturgy that Schmemann would remember most. However, Bulgakov's theological creativity produced a backlash from more conservative groups such as the Russian Orthodox Church Abroad, who condemned his writings on the notion of the divine wisdom or "sophiology."[46] Bulgakov had written that the divine wisdom was not separate from God but was a feminine principle within the Godhead, which was distinctly manifested in Scripture. Bulgakov's theological reflection on wisdom instigated his colleagues to have him expelled from teaching theology. Yet—as both Plekon and Valliere observe—Bulgakov himself was never condemned as a heretic, and his books and articles continue to enjoy a large readership today.[47]

---

45. Silk, "The Eucharistic Revival Movement in the Orthodox Church in America," 26.

46. See Bryan Geffert "The Charges of Heresy against Sergii Bulkagov," *St. Vladimir's Seminary Theological Quarterly* 49 No. 1-2 (2005): 47-66.

47. See Paul Valliere, *Modern Russian Theology* (Grand Rapids, MI: Eerdmans, 2000), 10.

Certainly these are not the only persons who influenced Schmemann. Yet these three—Afanasiev, Kern, and Bulgakov—seem to stand out in Schmemann's own writings; it is clear through allusions direct and indirect that each one of them greatly impacted Schmemann's thinking about the Eucharist. In the classroom Schmemann learned from them the importance of the pastoral nature of liturgy, by attending lectures by Bulgakov and attending the weekly liturgies, by serving at Sts. Constantine and Helen Church with Kyprian Kern, as well as interacting with his colleague John Meyendorff.

While these three men had differing thoughts and ideas about the Church, they were all very much dedicated to the building up of the Body of Christ, and saw the liturgy as the foundation for this building. It was their common devotion to the Eucharist that inspired Schmemann's own thoughts about the role and function of the Eucharist in the life of the Church.

Chapter 3

Alexander Schmemann and Pastoral Liturgy

Before beginning a discussion of Schmemann's liturgical theology, a brief note must be made about the importance and impact of the Liturgical Reform Movement in the Roman Catholic Church, which also influenced Fr. Schmemann. We cannot understand Schmemann's pastoral theology without an understanding of his liturgical theology.

It was providential that Schmemann lived and studied in Paris during the early part of the 20th century. Not only was Europe the center of the Russian religious renaissance, but also of the much larger, ecumenical Liturgical Movement. The Liturgical Movement was like the Paris School revival, in that it was not one large organized group, but comprised of a general interest in liturgical renewal. Like the Paris School, it is difficult to date the Liturgical Movement, since its antecedents are toward the end of the 19th century, and some scholars argue that in certain circles, the work of the Liturgical Movement continues.

Schmemann does not specifically mention the impact that the Liturgical Movement had on his thought, although he often mentions Gregory Dix, osb, Odo Casel, osb, Jean Daniélou, sj, and Bernard Botte, osb, in his writings. While much has been said about the historical development of the Liturgical Movement in Europe and the United States, I want to emphasize the pastoral nature of the liturgy, as seen by the Liturgical Movement.[1]

---

1. See Andre Haquin "The Liturgical Movement and the Catholic Ritual Revision," in Geoffrey Wainwright and Karen B. Westerfield Tucker, eds., *The Oxford History of Christian Worship* (New York: Oxford University Press, 2006), 696–721.

The Liturgical Movement was directed toward increasing the participation of the laity in worship, providing educational and catechetical materials for both clergy and laity, and emphasizing the importance of the Eucharist for spiritual life and development. The historical study of the liturgy was the foundation for the pastoral thrust of the movement. In other words, the historical study of the liturgy provided fertile soil so that the pastoral reforms could bear fruit.

The Liturgical Movement produced new translations of the liturgy into the vernacular, especially French, German, and Italian. The leaders of the Liturgical Movement also supported frequent reception of Holy Communion, which was as unusual in the Catholic Church at the time as it was in the Orthodox Church. In most parishes of either Church, people would usually receive Communion on Christmas or Easter, and perhaps during the season of Great Lent.

The work of the Liturgical Movement bore fruit not only in Europe but in North America as well. As clergy and theologians came to the United States around the turn of the century, they brought with them their experiences of liturgical renewal in Europe. The works of Alcuin Deutsch, OSB, Virgil Michel, OSB, Reynold Hillenbrand, Martin Hellreigel, and Godfrey Diekmann, OSB, have made an indelible mark on the liturgical revival within the Catholic Church in North America. Their combined efforts helped to bring the laity into a fuller understanding of what it means to be members of one another, and to offer a common prayer and praise to God in the local language. The publication of the journal *Orates Fratres*, begun by Michel and the monks at St. John's Abbey in Collegeville, Minnesota, which was subsequently renamed *Worship*, was an important contribution to the academic and pastoral expression of liturgy. The establishment of Liturgical Press out of the same abbey was another important component of the Liturgical Movement, since it provided both scholarly and popular publications for lay education and for use in parish worship. Liturgical Press is one of the many Catholic publishers that now provide resources for parish and pastoral use, especially in the area of liturgical theology and renewal.

The Liturgical Movement was certainly a very important part of the history of theological development in the Catholic Church. However, one cannot downplay the impact that the Liturgical

Movement had on Schmemann. His time in Paris put him in contact with the ideas not only of the Orthodox scholars mentioned in the last chapter, but also those of Roman Catholic scholars, with whom he had much in common.

Liturgical Theology: *Theologia Prima*

One very important by-product that arose from the Liturgical Movement was a renewed academic and pastoral interest in liturgy. The liturgical reformers understood that liturgy was more than an analysis of rites and rituals, what some called liturgiology. Louis Bouyer (among others) emphasized that liturgy was more than an object of theological study or even a sub-field of theology, but rather a source for theology or a foundation from which theology flows. In his book *Liturgical Piety*, Bouyer draws an important distinction between the theology of the liturgy and liturgical theology:

> Let us now turn to the theological study of liturgy. Here we must first make a most important distinction. The theology of the liturgy is the science which begins with the liturgy itself in order to give a theological explanation of what the liturgy is, and of what is implied in its rites and words. Those authors are not to be accounted as liturgical theologians, therefore, who go to work the other way round and seek to impose on liturgy a ready-made explanation which pays little or no attention to what liturgy says about itself. We must emphasize this distinction, since such a mistaken method of theologizing about the liturgy was not born today or even yesterday.[2]

Bouyer makes a very important comment concerning the shift in meaning from the "theology of the liturgy" to "liturgical theology." The former practice viewed the liturgy primarily in its symbolism— from processions to prayers and blessings—from which one could derive meaning. However, liturgy is more than an "object" or "subject" about which one can theologize, but rather provides its own theology. In other words, the liturgy provides meaning in and of itself. Schmemann would later write, "Liturgical theology, on the other hand, is based upon the recognition that the liturgy in its totality is

---

2. Louis Bouyer, *Liturgical Piety* (Notre Dame, IN: University of Notre Dame Press, 1978) 277.

not only an 'object' of theology, but above all its source, and this by
virtue of the liturgy's essential function, *i.e.*, that of revealing by the
means which are proper to it (and by which belong only to it) the faith
of the church; in other words, of being that the *lex orandi* in which the
lex credendi finds its principal criterion and standard."[3]

However, for reformers like Bouyer and Schmemann, the
primary function for liturgical studies had to be on the historical level,
since this is where the fundamental structures could be found.
Schmemann himself notes that historical analysis of the liturgy will
always be necessary. After all, an understanding of the historical
development of liturgical rites, rituals, and what Schmemann called
the "*ordo*" is requisite for reflection on the theological importance of
what worship is saying to the faithful.[4] The underlying textual meaning of the liturgical prayers, symbols, and rites must be understood
before the overarching message can be derived. However,
Schmemann, like many Roman Catholic Church reformers, wanted
more than to understand the rites as they were received and practiced
in the Church, but to get to the very message of worship itself.
Schmemann developed his vision of liturgical theology in a scholarly
exchange with the late Bernard Botte and W. Jardine Grisbrooke.
At one point in his essay "Liturgical Theology, Theology of Liturgy,
and Liturgical Reform," Schmemann emphatically states:

> But then liturgical theology—and I cannot overemphasize this—is not
> the that part of theology, that "discipline," which deals with liturgy
> "in itself," has liturgy as its specific "object," but first of all and above
> everything else, the attempt to grasp the "theology" as revealed in and
> through liturgy. There is, I maintain, a radical and indeed irreducible
> difference between these two approaches to liturgical theology whose task
> then obviously depends whether one opts for the one or the other . . .
> In the approach which I advocate by every line I ever wrote, the question
> addressed by liturgical theology to liturgy and to the entire liturgical

---

3. Schmemann, "Liturgy Theology: Remarks on Method" in Thomas Fisch, ed., *Liturgy and Tradition: Theological Reflections of Alexander Schmemann* (Crestwood, NY: St. Vladimir's Seminary Press, 1990), 138.

4. Schmemann's doctoral dissertation was published with the title *Introduction to Liturgical Theology* (Crestwood, NY: St. Vladimir's Seminary Press, 1966). Schmemann explains in great detail the development of the *ordo* throughout the centuries, ending with what he calls the Byzantine synthesis.

Tradition is not about liturgy but about "theology," i.e., about the faith of the Church as expressed, communicated and preserved by the liturgy . . .[5]

In the above passage, Schmemann emphasizes that theology transmits not an abstract truth, but rather the truth of the Gospel message, which is one of salvation, fulfilled and nourished in the celebration of the Eucharistic liturgy. In a discussion on Schmemann's liturgical theology, David Fagerberg states,

> Liturgical theology's ultimate concern is not with texts as resources, but with the Church's living faith itself. Questions about the liturgical *ordo* are penultimate to the theological issue that ultimately concerns the liturgical theologian. Since the meaning of liturgy is God's act upon God's people, its interpretation is nothing less than the elucidation of the mystery of the divinely bestowed new life, *i.e.,* theology.[6]

Fagerberg continues by reminding his readers that the ultimate aim of liturgy is "talk about God," because liturgy concerns itself with the "reign of God, the kingdom at hand, the life of adoption, Christ among us, redeemed life, eschatological existence."[7] This is what Kavanagh and others would call *theologia prima*, or primary theology. Primary theology speaks directly of God, while *theologia secunda* are theological abstractions or academic reflections about God, what is sometimes called scholastic or "school" theology. Unfortunately, pastors and professors often engage in *theologia secunda* in place of *theologia prima*. In his book *Introduction to Liturgical Theology*, Kavanagh comments on the understanding of liturgical theology as *theologia prima*:

> It is also to argue that doing liturgical theology comes closer to doing *theologia prima* than *theologia secunda* or a "theology of the liturgy," and that doing primary theology places a whole set of requirements on the theologian which are not quite the same as those placed on a theologian who does only secondary theology. For what emerges most directly from an assembly's liturgical act is not a new species of theology among others. It is *theologia* itself.[8]

---

5. Ibid., 40.

6. David Fagerberg *Theologia Prima: What is Liturgical Theology?* (Chicago/Mundelein, IL: Hillenbrand Books, 2004), 81.

7. Ibid.

8. Aidan Kavanagh, *On Liturgical Theology* (Collegeville, MN: Pueblo, 1992), 75.

While *theologia secunda* has its place in the academy, it is not life-giving, it does not adequately express true theology as does *theologia prima*; therefore, *theologia secunda* should never dominate over *theologia prima*. Unfortunately, *theologia secunda* generally does dominate the academy, and further adds to the reduction of liturgy to merely rites and rubrics, which consequently leads to a reduction of other areas in the Church such as ministry, preaching, and pastoral care:

> Ministry changes from consecrated service to communities of faith into a profession, then a trade, and finally into an avocation for some and a series of options for others. Homiletics becomes less the hearing of the gospel out loud, so to speak, among one's peers in faith than an occasion for the certified to educated the uncertified about "issues" through argumentation, syllabi, and oratorical tricks. Sacraments diminish as unsettling encounters between living presences divine and human in the here and now, to become a rather abstract ritual expression of a pattern set by Christ to give scope to the universal Kingdom.[9]

Schmemann naturally placed greater emphasis on the *theologia prima*, rather than *theologia secunda* or theology of the liturgy. When the Church gathers for prayer and thanksgiving, the congregation experiences a liturgical act of the Church that is more than mere rites and rituals, but is true theology, as was emphasized by the earlier liturgists of the Liturgical Movement. As we hear God's Word and receive his broken Body and spilled Blood, we are receiving Christ himself who comes and makes his home with us; or as the Gospel according to John actually says, "has made his dwelling among us" (Jn 1:14). Every time we join the liturgical gathering, we are once again meeting God face to face. Jesus is Emmanuel, God-with-us, and as God he draws his people into a covenant with the Father, which is renewed and enlivened at every Eucharistic liturgy. God once again calls us to be his chosen people, and gives us the food of eternal life. Our response should be to hear that call and follow it.

Following God is not easy. It is done in a spirit of fear and trembling. When Isaiah encountered God's throne he immediately realized his sinfulness and said that he was "a man of unclean lips" (Is 6:5). Isaiah encountered the glory of God, his divine presence, the *shekinah* of God. The liturgical gathering is the forum where we speak

---

9. Ibid., 83.

to God as we offer a common hymn of praise, and where he speaks to us through his divine Word and the offering of his Son. We commune with true life itself, as is seen in the hymns following the distribution of holy Communion, "We have seen the true light! We have received the heavenly Spirit! We have found the true Faith! Worshipping the undivided Trinity, who has saved us."[10] Thus the liturgical gathering is the place where we meet God not face to face as Adam did, but through the hearing of the Good News, the Gospel, and in the partaking of the bread and wine, Christ's broken Body and spilled Blood. Worship is where God chooses to meet his people; it is a holy encounter between Him and us.

There is a story about how the Russians adopted Orthodox Christianity. When Prince Vladimir, then a pagan potentate, wanted to adopt a new religion, he sent his ambassadors throughout the far reaches of the world to learn more about the various religions. Some went to the Far East and learned about Buddhism and Hinduism, others went to the Middle East and learned about Islam, and others still went to Constantinople and learned about Orthodox Christianity. When the ambassadors returned back to Kiev to see Prince Vladimir they reported to him what they encountered. The ambassadors from Constantinople said that when they attended the Divine Liturgy they didn't know whether they were on earth or in heaven. The worship they encountered was so otherworldly and transcendent that it revealed the true mystery of the faith.

This story is perhaps more legendary than factual; we really do not know how Vladimir chose the Orthodox Christian faith over other religious beliefs. However, attending an Orthodox liturgical service—complete with incense, *a capella* singing, icons, processions, bread and wine, and oil, not to mention the blessing of water at the feast of Epiphany and other various services and blessings—emphasizes the symbolic nature of worship, that through the material and the earthly we encounter the holy and the divine, that liturgy truly is where earth and heaven meet. Geoffrey Wainwright, a contemporary liturgical theologian, states that even the icons seem to take part in the liturgy, since they depict the saints: the holy men and women, the

---

10. *Divine Liturgy of St. John Chrysostom*, 2nd Ed., (South Canaan, PA: St. Tikhon's Seminary Press, 1977).

martyrs, prophets, patriarchs, and Apostles, who "ascend to heaven, elevated and lifted up by Christ to his table in the kingdom."[11]

It is in the liturgical gathering of the Church that we are shaped and formed into the Body of Christ, and in which he dwells and makes his home among us. The liturgy is the forum where we call upon God and he speaks to us, and where we encounter true theology, words adequate to God. Thus, the true theologian is Kavanagh's Mrs. Murphy, who comes to Church every Sunday and breaks bread with her fellow congregants, who prays the prayers of the Church, offering thanksgiving to God.[12] Mrs. Murphy, like so many other parishioners, is living the life of faith—those in the academy may reflect and write about it, but Mrs. Murphy lives it. This very liturgical theology, true theology or speech about God, takes precedence over theology of the liturgy or *theologia secunda*:

> Theology is talk about God in self-revealing action, and liturgical theology can be considered genuine theology because God acts in the liturgy. The reason why liturgical theology unpacks the faith of the Church is because in the liturgy the Church experiences itself as the handiwork of God. Here, God's creative proclamation is manifested and faith is actualized. Liturgy, then, is not just a resource for theology, but its root.[13]

This encounter with God leads us to a serious recognition of our sinfulness, just as the moment Isaiah saw God's throne, he cried, "Woe is me, I am doomed! For I am a man of unclean lips . . ." (Is 6:5). When the myrrh-bearing women went to the tomb on the first day of the week and they encountered the angel of the Lord, a divine messenger, their first reaction was one of fear and trembling. It certainly is an awesome thing to encounter one of God's messengers. However we are guided and led in the Spirit to repent, or change our ways, repentance must be a complete change, a *metanoia*, a change of mind and a change of heart. The liturgy reminds us that we are sinners living with sinners, but all are washed and made clean through the blood of the Lamb and are seated at his banquet table. When we

---

11. Geoffrey Wainwright, "Christian Worship: Scriptural Basis and Theological Frame," in *The Oxford History of Christian Worship* (New York: Oxford University Press, 2006), 15.

12. For further clarification between *theologia prima* and *theologia secunda*, and Kavanagh's beloved Mrs. Murphy, see Robert F. Taft, "Mrs. Murphy Goes to Moscow: Kavanagh, Schmemann, and 'The Byzantine Synthesis,'" *Worship* 85, no. 5 (2011): 386–407.

13. Fagerberg, *Theologia Prima*, 81.

come into contact with the holiness of God, we are transformed, and in so doing, we are called to bring this holiness to the world in which we live, what Chrysostom called "living the liturgy after the liturgy," a term that Schmemann often uses in his writing.[14] This other "liturgy" is where we encounter the person of Christ in our neighbor, and we respond by showing and expressing unconditional love.[15] At the conclusion of the Roman liturgy, the priest dismisses the congregation to "Go in peace," which is not just a nice way of saying goodbye, but is a command to go back into the world and bring the peace, love, and grace of God to the world in which we live. Christians are called to live in a continually grace-filled life, and are fed and nourished by both Word and Bread to enable them to live this life. Thus the liturgy should be a constant reminder that we too are called to be holy, to live according to the will of God, to love our neighbors as ourselves.[16]

Schmemann repeats his vision of the Eucharist, which both unifies the Church in its role as the Body of Christ and functions as the source for theology. Following in the footsteps of Afanasiev, Schmemann regards the Eucharist as constituting the Church itself, which can only fully be the Church when its members gather together for the praise and prayer that is fulfilled in the Eucharistic liturgy:

> Furthermore, while the Eucharist must unquestionably be placed in the center of the first part of liturgical theology, the essential nature of the Church being actualized in the Eucharist as the sacrament of the Church's life, it is also true that the sacraments of the entrance into the Church (Baptism and Chrismation) lead us into this life and unite us with this essential nature. They lead into the Church and into the

---

14. See also Ion Bria, *The Liturgy after the Liturgy* (Geneva, Switzerland: World Council of Churches, 1996).

15. David Fagerberg observed that the Church adopted the word *leitourgia* to name her cult. See Fagerberg, *Theologia Prima*, 12. Schmemann also usually renders the term "liturgy" in the original Greek: *leitourgia*. This rendering is not by accident or in terms of style, but Schmemann's way of emphasizing the fact that worship is truly the work of God's people—which is the primary meaning of liturgy, a public act or work. Therefore, the phrase "the liturgy after the liturgy" refers to our work in the world, as we bring the joy, peace, and love of the Kingdom to those around us, which is our participation in the work of God in the world, as co-creators with God.

16. This theme of the "liturgy after the liturgy," or the social implications of the liturgy, is repeated by other Orthodox writers, including Mother Maria Skobtsova, Paul Evdokimov, Sergius Bulgakov, and Anton Kartashev. They all saw the need of living the liturgical life in the world around them through the care and service of others. They were against any "liturgical reductionism" that would separate Church from world or liturgy from life. For them, as for many other Orthodox thinkers, liturgy and life were one seamless whole.

Eucharist, and it is appropriate to relate their theological and liturgical explanation to the study of the celebration of the Eucharist itself.[17]

Schmemann therefore sees the Eucharist as the action that both unifies and fulfills worship. Furthermore, the Eucharistic liturgy transforms the reality of daily existence, providing the transformation of life into the presence of God's Kingdom, as seen in the following commentary by Plekon:

> The whole of the day, the night, the year, all of time is sanctified in the liturgy. All of human activity is to be transformed: work, play, eating, sleeping. Every point in human life is a moment of God's saving and bringing us back: from our burial and resurrection in Baptism, to Chrismation, or Confirmation, to Christian marriage, the anointing of the sick, and the burial of the Christian. Through the Church's liturgy and ordained ministry all of human life, especially material things— bread, wine, oil, water, words, touch—are directed back to what they were created to be—good in God's sight and, in the case of humankind, his very image and likeness. The consequence of this life of God and with God in liturgy is made explicit. Time becomes the very "sacrament of the world to come," the eschatological icon of God's saving and reclaiming of his fallen creation . . . Father Schmemann constantly emphasized the paschal or resurrectional nature of the Church, the liturgy, and Christian living, an intense realization within the Eastern Church's experience, exemplified by numerous holy women and men even in our own era.[18]

This clear connection between what we say in the prayers and how the Church worships is very important. When referring to the nature of worship in the Church, Schmemann would use the abbreviated Latin phrase: *lex orandi, lex credendi*, which can be translated, "let the rule of prayer establish the rule of faith." The phrase was a reduction of a lengthier statement made by the theologian Prosper of Aquitaine (d. 463 AD): "*ut legem credendi lex statuat supplicandi.*"[19] The phrase asserts that faith or belief comes through worship, that in and through worship one comes into contact with the divine, and thus begins to grow toward the knowledge of God. Kavanagh reflects on the notion

---

17. Alexander Schmemann, *Introduction to Liturgical Theology* (Crestwood, NY: St. Vladimir's Seminary Press, 1987), 25.

18. Plekon, *Living Icons*, 190.

19. Kavanagh, *On Liturgical Theology*, 46.

of *lex orandi, lex credendi* in his comments on Augustine's conversion to Christianity:

> Christians do not succumb to the grace of faith first and then sort out what their options for worship might be. Augustine worshipped with the faithful for years before he finally succumbed to the grace of faith, as he tells us, on the occasion of hearing a child's voice singing in the distance "Take and read, take and read." What he read was the Bible which he had already heard read in worship over and over again since he himself was a child, and more lately heard preached in public worship by the great Ambrose of Milan. Throughout Augustine's own life as a rather wandering catechumen for thirty years, he had been deeply enfolded by the church's *lex supplicandi*.[20]

Thus the phrase *lex orandi, lex credendi* leads Schmemann to comment on the importance of the Eucharist in the life of the Church. According to Schmemann, the Eucharist is the source and foundation of all of the fasts, feast days, saints' days, prayers, blessings, hymns, and celebrations of the Church. Everything in the Church has the Eucharist at its center. In his essay "Theology and Eucharist," Schmemann elaborated on this Eucharistic vision in regards to an earlier approach that was common in both the Western and Eastern theological traditions:

> In the official, post-patristic and "Westernizing" theology, the Eucharist is treated as merely one of the sacraments. Its place in ecclesiology is that of "means of grace"—one among many. However central and essential in the life of the Church, the Eucharist is institutionally distinct from the Church. It is the power, the grace given to the Church that makes the Eucharist possible, valid, efficient, but this power of grace "precedes" the Eucharist and is virtually independent from it. Thus the Church is understood and described here as an institution endowed with divine power: power to teach, to guide, to sanctify, as a structure for the communication of grace; a "power," however, which is not derived from the Eucharist. The latter is a fruit, a result of the Church, not her source.[21]

Schmemann took this Eucharistic vision—formed during the years of the Liturgical Movement in Paris, fostered and fertilized by Western liturgists including Bouyer and Daniélou—and brought it to the

---

20. Ibid., 98.
21. Ibid., 72.

Orthodox Church in America. It is in the United States that Schmemann developed and spread his liturgical vision as a means toward renewal and reform in the understanding and meaning of worship.

Pastoral Nature of Liturgy

Schmemann's critics have questioned his approach to liturgy and have pointed out that he emphasized liturgical worship over spirituality, outreach to the poor and needy, and mission and evangelism. However, when reading Schmemann's theological corpus *in toto*, one actually sees an intimate connection between liturgy and life. According to Schmemann, liturgy is meant to be missionary, in that liturgy always proclaims the Gospel to the world around us. As mission, the liturgy is called to transform both the worshipping community and the culture and society in which we live. Therefore, if we take liturgy seriously we will in fact take evangelism, missionary work, and service to the poor seriously as well. This missionary and transformative nature of the Eucharistic liturgy was the topic for reflection of this journal entry of Schmemann's from early 1973:

> The Eucharist reveals the Church as community—love for Christ, love in Christ—as a mission to turn each and all to Christ. The Church has no other purpose, no "religious life" separate from the world. Otherwise the Church would become an idol. The Church is the home each of us leaves to go to work and to which one returns with joy in order to find life, happiness and joy, to which everyone brings back the fruits of his labor and where everything is transformed into a feast, into freedom and fulfillment, the presence, the experience of this "home"—already out of time, unchanging, filled with eternity, revealing eternity. Only this presence can give meaning and value to everything in life, can refer everything to that experience and make it full. "The image of this world is passing away." But only by passing away does the world finally become the "World": a gift of God, a happiness that comes from being in communion with the content, the form, the image of that "World."[22]

The liturgy then becomes a mission to the world, as the faithful are called to bring the love, joy, peace, and blessedness of the Kingdom to

---

22. Schmemann, *Journals*, 25.

the world, as the risen Lord commanded his disciples, "Go, therefore, and make disciples of all nations, baptizing them in the name of the Father, and of the Son, and of the holy Spirit, teaching them to observe all that I have commanded you. And behold, I am with you always, until the end of the age" (Mt 28:19–20). Following our Lord's injunction to continue his teaching ministry, the Church of God is called to continue this proclamation of the Good News of salvation to whoever has ears to hear.

The liturgy challenges us to become missionaries of the Good News to the entire world, in order to see life as transformed in the eyes of God. In other words, we are to live the life of the Kingdom in the "here and now," always seeking to incarnate the love, peace, and joy of the Kingdom in our daily relationships with friends and family, co-workers, and neighbors. The transformative nature of worship was a theme for reflection in another of Schmemann's writings:

> One of Osip Mandelstam's poems, devoted to the Eucharistic liturgy, the main service of Christian worship, includes this wonderful verse: "Take into your hands the whole world, as if it were a simple apple . . ." In an apple, and in everything within the world, faith sees, recognizes, and accepts God's gift, filled with love, beauty and wisdom. Faith hears the apple and the world speaking of that boundless love that created the world and life and gave them to us as our life. The world itself is the fruit of God's love for humanity, and only through the world can human beings recognize God and love him in return . . . And only in truly loving his own life, can a person thereby accept the life of the world as God's gift. Our fall, our sin is that we take everything for granted—and therefore everything, including ourselves, becomes routine, depressing, empty. The apple becomes just an apple. Bread is just bread. A human being is just a human being. We know their weight, their appearance, their activities, we know everything about them, we no longer know them, because we do not see the light that shines through them. The eternal task of faith and of the Church is to overcome this sinful, monotonous habituation; to enable us to see once again what we have forgotten how to see, to feel what we no longer feel; to experience what we are no longer capable of experiencing. Thus, the priest blesses bread and wine, lifting them up to heaven, but faith sees the bread of life, it sees sacrifice and gift, it sees communion with life eternal.[23]

23. Alexander Schmemann, *Celebration of Faith, Vol. 2: The Church Year*, trans. John Jillions (Crestwood, NY: St. Vladimir's Seminary Press, 1997), 160–161.

In the above passage Schmemann outlines his thoughts on all of life as a liturgical service, that the work of worship is to see everything already transformed and transfigured by the love of God. At its very core, liturgy reminds us that all of life is sacred, that spirituality is found in everyday objects—bread, wine, oil—and is expressed through the stages of birth, Baptism, marriage, and death. Authentic spirituality is none other than communion with the God of all creation who makes himself known in the breaking of the bread and in the sharing of fellowship with one another (Lk 24:13ff). Throughout his lifetime Schmemann railed against separating liturgy from life, the Church from the world, the world from the Kingdom; for Schmemann there is only the life of God, and this life is holy, sacred, and good. All of life has been redeemed, sanctified, and offered up to God through Christ on the cross, and is celebrated and memorialized in the Eucharistic celebration, as the Book of Revelation says, "Behold, I make all things new" (Rv 21:5).

Woven throughout his writings on liturgical theology is Schmemann's belief that, at its very foundation, liturgy must be first and foremost for the salvation of souls, since the liturgy is where we encounter God, who is primarily interested in our salvation. Thus, while it is important to understand the meaning and historical development of the rites, rubrics, or *ordo* of the liturgy, the foundation of the liturgy is our salvation. The feasts, fasts, saints' days, sacraments, and mysteries not only mark our life in Christ from birth to death, but are encounters with the Kingdom of Heaven. The community of faith enters a new reality as it meets the living God in the liturgical gathering.

Conclusion

Placing Schmemann's career within the larger context of both the Paris School and the Liturgical Movement (first in Europe and then in the United States) demonstrates clearly that Schmemann was theologically formed during a period of liturgical renewal and reform in both the Western and Eastern Churches, which contributed much to his role in cultivating a liturgical renaissance here in the United States. Schmemann gleaned insights from each of the many scholars he encountered, regardless of religious background, and applied them to the pastoral needs he saw firsthand.

His work as a pastor and as dean at St. Vladimir's Seminary provided opportunities for Schmemann to spread his liturgical vision of the Church to hundreds—if not thousands—of people, both clergy and laity. Schmemann always managed to keep this vision in front of him, whether he was speaking to a meeting of Orthodox bishops at the Holy Synod, an international gathering of theologians, or the congregation in the pews on Sunday.

Before turning to Schmemann's vision of the Eucharist, we must consider Schmemann's emphasis on Baptism, since it is in Baptism that the Christian enters into the Death of Jesus Christ, is raised to new life, and becomes a member of the Body of Christ and a sharer in his royal priesthood.

Part II

Baptism and Orders: Portals to Pastoral Theology

Chapter 4

Theological Foundations of Baptism

Schmemann's vision of pastoral theology is clearly underpinned by his understanding both of Baptism and Chrismation (in the West, Confirmation), which form the rites of initiation into the life of Christ, and of the Eucharist, which is the fulfillment of that initiation.[1] These three rites—Baptism, Chrismation, and Eucharist—are the foundation of the Christian life, and they form the beginning point of our entrance into the Church. Furthermore, Baptism provides a context for understanding priestly ministry and its connection with the Eucharist. Baptism makes a person a member of the royal priesthood of all believers; thus through Baptism and Chrismation, Schmemann taught, we are in a sense "ordained," or set apart for God's work in the world, and become part of the royal priesthood of God's Kingdom. The holy orders of deacon, priest, and bishop set men apart for a more formalized ministry within the Church.

Beginning with Baptism

Schmemann begins the discussion of ecclesial life and pastoral theology with a reflection on the sacrament of Baptism, which is the liturgical and sacramental entrance into the community of faith. Very often we speak of Baptism in association with the other sacraments of Chrismation and Eucharist. In the Eastern Church, each liturgical rite flows organically and naturally into the next: the child or catechumen first enters into holy Baptism through the font, then he or she is given the gift of the Holy Spirit through the anointing with chrism,

---

1. Alexander Schmemann, *Eucharist* (Crestwood, NY: St. Vladimir's Seminary Press, 2003), 27.

and finally he or she receives Holy Communion, which is the culmination and fulfillment of the rites of entrance into the Church.
All three sacraments together form the way that a person is made
a Christian; as Tertullian was known to say, "Christians are made,
not born" (*Apology*, xvii). These sacraments are foundational to
Schmemann's view of pastoral theology, for they are the way in
which the Church expresses the life of God to the people of God.
For Schmemann, the Eucharist is a journey to the Kingdom of
God, and Baptism and Chrismation are the entrance to the road to
that Kingdom.

Schmemann begins his discussion on Baptism by decon-
structing how the sacrament of Baptism was viewed in his younger
years. At that time, in both Russia and Europe, Baptisms were family
events that did not include the parish community, which demonstrates
a clear dichotomy between the practice of Baptism and the way in
which the Church envisioned Baptism in its own liturgical structures
and rites. Baptisms generally took place only with a handful of people
present—the priest, the parents and godparents, and a few close
family friends.[2] Others were occasionally invited to witness the
Baptism, but there was very little understanding of the connection
between the Baptism and the Sunday Eucharist:

> Thus today, it takes some fifteen minutes to perform in a dark corner of a
> church, with one psalmist giving the responses, an act in which the
> Fathers saw and acclaimed the greatest solemnity of the Church . . . such
> is the sad situation in which we find ourselves today and which must be
> corrected if we love the Church and want her to become again the power
> which transforms the life of man.[3]

This privatization of the sacraments—seen not only in Baptism but
also in marriage and even the Eucharist—was a major problem in
Schmemann's time, not only within Orthodox circles but also in most
Roman Catholic, Lutheran, and Episcopal parishes. People attended
the Eucharistic service, but the emphasis on private prayer and
spiritual devotions usually took precedence over the liturgical action

---

2. For more details about the privatization of these sacramental acts, see Meyendorff,
"Fr. Alexander Schmemann's Liturgical Legacy in America," *St. Vladimir's Theological Quarterly*
53, no. 2–3 (2009): 319–330, especially note 4 on page 323.

3. Schmemann, *Of Water and Spirit* (Crestwood, NY: St. Vladimir's Seminary Press, 2000), 11.

of the Divine Liturgy. Kern's summation of this sacramental reductionism is particularly keen:

> [I]n our time Eucharistic life is weakened to the point that we have almost completely lost the proper Eucharistic consciousness, and regard the Divine Liturgy being celebrated in our churches as just one of the ceremonies, considering secondary devotional services as no less important in worship . . .[4]

Kern goes on to say that this continual privatization has negatively influenced all of ecclesial life, reducing to personal and private concerns what should be focused on the Body of Christ, which always presupposes a community or *ecclesia*. Schmemann saw this privatization as detracting from the ecclesial reality of the sacramental life, in that the Christian life is a continual preparation for eternal life, and that this preparation must take place within a community of faith, not apart from it:

> We must realize first of all that preparation is a constant and essential aspect of the Church's worship as a whole. It is impossible to enter into the spirit of liturgy, to understand its meaning and truly to participate in it without first understanding that it is built primarily on the double rhythm of preparation and fulfillment, and that this rhythm is essential to the Church's liturgy because it reveals and indeed fulfills the double nature and function of the Church herself.[5]

While there is a place for private prayer and devotional practices like *lectio divina* and spiritual meditation, the Eucharistic offering is an ecclesial and communal event. The celebration of the Eucharist is not the place for private prayer, it is the gathering of the people of God around the altar of the Lord, joining with the great choirs of angels and saints, including those who have preceded us in death. Schmemann always emphasized the communal nature of the sacraments; they are the vehicle through which the community of faith prays and worships. This participation in the paschal elements of the faith, the Death and saving Resurrection of Christ, is a passage—or Passover—from death to life, and is truly a rebirth.

---

4. Schmemann, *Introduction to Liturgical Theology* (Crestwood, NY: St. Vladimir's Seminary Press, 1966), 25.

5. Ibid., 16.

In some places the practice of Baptism has changed little. Some clergy and laity still see Baptism as merely fulfilling a religious or ritual obligation to the parish. It is not uncommon for parents to request private Baptisms with only the parents and godparents present; furthermore, they see no need for a Baptism on a Sunday during the Eucharistic liturgy with the entire community present.

Another pastoral problem with Baptism that Schmemann identifies is parents who participate in the external celebration of Baptism without seeking an inward conversion—in other words, the baptismal service occurs with no real incarnation in the hearts of the family. In many parishes today, as in Schmemann's time, it was difficult for some people to internalize the message of the prayers, Scripture readings, and actions to understand what is taking place during the rite. Some parents come to the Church with deep sincerity and conviction to have their child baptized because that is the normal or expected thing to do, but they do not allow the hymns, prayers, and Scripture lessons to permeate their hearts and minds—they do not allow the liturgy to take root. Without interior participation in the sacraments, it is difficult to live out the faith. A family can attend services on a routine basis, say rote prayers, and make financial offerings, and still have these actions be merely external; the rubrics and form of the sacraments have little or no connection to their lives without interior devotion.

Schmemann's response to this reductionist understanding of Baptism is sound liturgical preaching and teaching. For Schmemann, the Church must convey the importance of the rites and rituals of the faith, starting with the initiatory rites of Baptism and Chrismation. Our life in Christ begins at Baptism; thus it ought to supply for us a firm foundation upon which we can build our lives. The Lectionary provides a wellspring of lessons on Baptism; through the ordinary proclamation of the Scriptures, priests can bring to the fore the importance of Baptism. Likewise, the Church year itself—especially the feasts of Epiphany, Easter, and Pentecost—offers many wonderful examples of renewing of our lives in Christ through water and the Spirit. The Collects, chants, and prayers of these festivals supply ample material to inspire such preaching and teaching.[6] Other

---

6. For example, a colleague of mine once told me that he always tries to mention the importance of Baptism in his sermons as a reminder that the entire Gospel message of salvation

avenues of formation are available to clergy, including seasonal retreats on the topic of Christian initiation, bulletin articles, and talks and presentations, both formal and informal. Baptism may be the beginning of our life in Christ, but it certainly should not be forgotten.[7]

Therefore, one of the major tasks of the priest is to help the laity remember their own Baptism and entrance into the Church. This is difficult, of course, because most adult Orthodox and Catholics today were baptized as infants, and thus we do not recall our own Baptism. Still, every time the priest reads the baptismal prayers, anoints with oil, and reads the Scripture lessons, we too are reminded of our life in Christ. The infant may be the one who is being baptized on a particular Sunday, but we too are renewing our baptismal vows.

Kavanagh draws upon the theological concept of *anamnesis*, or remembrance, as a way for the community of faith to enliven and relive their Baptism.[8] One of the most important ways for people to remember their Baptism is to hear about it often, whether in sermons, bulletins, or adult education classes. "A Christian of the past knew, for example that Easter each year was the celebration of his own Baptism, of his own entrance into and participation in the life of the Risen Christ. He knew that the Resurrection of Christ was again revealed and reaffirmed in this act of regeneration and rebirth through which new members were integrated into the 'newness of life.'"[9] *Anamnesis* is fundamental to understanding our own place in the Church. How many people who witness a marriage remember their own marriage at the ceremony? Or who attends a funeral of a friend or loved one and does not consider his or her own mortality? A constant sense of remembering brings to the forefront the reality that we are fully members of the Body of Christ who are being formed and shaped into the likeness of Christ. Once we stop remembering who we are, we stop functioning as members of the Body.

---

is based on our repentance, which begins in Baptism.

7. The parish in which I was raised has a beautiful icon of the baptism of Jesus Christ in the foyer or nave of the Church, where there was also a raised area on which the baptismal font was kept until it was brought into the center of the Church, where Baptisms occurred. Seeing the baptismal font every Sunday was a constant reminder of our own Baptism into Christ.

8. Aidan Kavanagh, *The Shape of Baptism: The Rite of Christian Initiation* (Collegeville, MN: Liturgical Press, 1991), 176.

9. Schmemann, *Of Water and the Spirit*, 8.

The Christian concept of remembrance stems from the ancient Hebrew understanding of the word, which means *to make present*. At every Passover meal the father of the house recalls the Exodus story and the deliverance that the Lord performed for his people. The act of remembering the Exodus story makes present God's saving power in today's world. Similarly, at every Baptism we are called to remember our own Baptism, and the prayers and symbolic actions once again become powerful for us. The people of God must identify ourselves with the child in the font, for just as he or she is accepting a new birth of water and the Spirit, so too are we accepting the same rebirth in our own lives: the coming of Christ to exorcize the demons from our lives, receiving sanctification and redemption through the baptismal waters, being clothed with the white garment of purity, accepting the call to walk in newness of life.

THE FOUNDATIONS OF BAPTISM

Baptism was a common cleansing ritual in the ancient world, symbolizing both renewal and regeneration; later it took on Christological meaning when the early Christians began baptizing in the name of Jesus. Likewise, many world religions have some type of water cleansing ritual as a path toward regeneration, renewal, and rebirth. [10] The Jews conducted routine rites of purification that included a water bath; whether they understood this as a life-changing moment is unknown. John the Baptist performed baptisms for the forgiveness of sins, but promised that another would come with a greater baptism: "I am baptizing you with water, for repentance, but the one who is coming after me is mightier than I. I am not worthy to carry his sandals. He will baptize you with the holy Spirit and fire" (Mt 3:11). Similarly, Jesus tells Nicodemus, "Amen, amen, I say to you, no one can enter the kingdom of God without being born of water and Spirit" (Jn 3:5).

It is this new life in Christ that makes us children of God, full and active members of his Body. Pastoral theology, in its very foundation, helps us to realize that each and every member of this Body is important and special, and that all are called to use our God-given talents for the building up of his Church. We are more

---

10. Ibid., 39.

than dues-paying members of a local congregation; we are adopted sons and daughters of God, washed clean in Baptism, and fed with his Body and Blood in the Eucharist. In his epistle to the Romans, the Apostle Paul writes: "Or are you unaware that we who were baptized into Christ Jesus were baptized into his death? We were indeed buried with him through Baptism into death, so that, just as Christ was raised from the dead by the glory of the Father, we too might live in newness of life" (Rom 6:3–4). Here Paul links Baptism with the Death of Jesus, and the hope of "new life" that this Death provides. Paul views Baptism not as merely a cleansing ritual, but as a symbolic participation in Christ's Death and, by extension, an entrance into the community of faith. In Baptism we die to the old Adam, the old man, the old fallen self that is still in us. Through the font, we die to this world and are raised as new creatures, endowed with love and passion for God. This redemptive nature of Baptism is seen in the prayers of the Eastern Church as the priest blesses the water:

> Wherefore, O Lord, manifest thyself in this water, and grant that he/she may put away from him/her the old man, which is corrupt through the lusts of the flesh, and that he/she may be clothed upon with the new man, and renewed after the image of him who created him/her: that being buried, after the pattern of thy death in Baptism, he/she may in like manner, be a partaker of thy Resurrection; and having preserved the gift of thy Holy Spirit, and increased the measure of grace committed unto him/her, he/she may receive the prize of his/her high calling, and be numbered with the first-born whose names are written in heaven, in thee, our God and Lord, Jesus Christ.[11]

In Baptism, newly initiated Christians turn their backs on their previous lives and enter a new life in Christ. The initiates put on Christ, as Paul states in his letter to the Galatians, "For all of you who were baptized into Christ have clothed yourselves with Christ" (Gal 3:27).[12] Clothing ourselves with Christ means that we are called to live the life that Christ offers to us, a life that is focused on repenting from our sins, striving for holiness, and being good stew-

---

11. "First Prayer of Exorcism," in Paul Lazor, editor, *Baptism* (New York: Department of Religions Education, The Orthodox Church of America, 1994), 33–34.

12. See also Col 2:12 and 1 Cor 12:13.

ards of the gifts that the Lord has provided for us. This reception of new life requires a commitment to live and walk according to God's commandments, living a life worthy of our calling as Christians— acting in a loving and charitable manner, and offering prayers and intercessions to God.

Chapter 5

Rite of Baptism as Entrance into the Royal Priesthood

Schmemann offered his readers a theological explanation of Baptism by analyzing the liturgical rites surrounding the baptismal service. As the historical development of these rites are quite complex, Schmemann bypasses this aspect in order to explain what is most beautifully expressed in the liturgical rites themselves. Some have accused him of poor scholarship and perhaps rightfully so.[1] However, one must also consider that he was writing not for other scholars per se, but for a broad, general readership. Schmemann recognized the contemporary lack of theological reflection on the liturgical rites and rituals that are the center of the sacramental life. The prayers and rites reveal the Gospel message—that God has come and has saved us through his Son Jesus—and the sacraments are symbols that reveal his salvation and life-creating grace. The Church would be better served if clergy and lay educators once again returned to the well-spring of our rich liturgical tradition as a source for catechesis, preaching, and teaching. The liturgy contains within itself everything that points to the Kingdom of God, a theme Schmemann emphasizes throughout his writings.

In the Orthodox liturgical tradition, the baptismal service contains three prayers of exorcism, which are followed by a confession of faith, the recitation of the Nicene Creed. The priest next performs the rite of pre-baptismal anointing of the child, then the great prayer of water blessing, which is immediately followed by the Baptism itself.

---

1. Peter Galazda "Schmemann between Fagerberg and Reality: Towards an Agenda for Byzantine Christian Pastoral Liturgy," in *Bolletina della Badia Greca di Grottaferrata terra* series 4 (2007): 7–32.

As the child is taken out of the baptismal font, the priest blesses the white gown and the cross. Then the child is anointed with holy chrism, a special oil mixed with various spices. It is common practice for the priest to anoint all of the senses: eyes, ears, throat, chest, hands, and feet. Then the child is carried around the baptismal font by his or her godparents three times, walking behind the priest who carries a hand cross. At the end of the service, the chrism is removed and then the child is given a tonsure, whereby the priest cuts small pieces of hair in the form of the cross on the child's head, symbolizing the child's first sacrifice to God.

The rite of Eastern Baptism includes a series of three prayers of exorcism, which recall the sin of Adam and fallen human nature. In Genesis we see that God made man and woman and he made them good (see Gn 1:26—2:25). However, because of pride, they disobeyed God's command not to eat of the fruit of the tree of knowledge of good and evil, and so they were exiled from Eden (see Gn 3). The following chapters tell a story of a fallen humanity, of man who, no longer in Eden, has to work hard and earn his bread "by the sweat of [his] face" (Gn 3:19).

The three exorcism prayers show us that while Jesus defeated death through his Crucifixion and Resurrection, evil and darkness still reign. While creation is good, as we know from the first chapter of Genesis, we also know that we live in a fallen world, where sin, suffering, pain, and evil still hold us captive. We just have to look around us to see brokenness in the world: poverty, orphaned and abandoned children, wars, epidemics, plagues, and natural disasters— not to mention the abuse of power and authority among our political leaders. Yet we also know that it is only the victory of Jesus that can defeat the powers and principalities that reign supreme: "Behold, I am coming soon. I bring with me the recompense I will give to each according to his deeds. I am the Alpha and the Omega, the first and the last, the beginning and the end" (Rv 22:12–13). Jesus is the one who destroys evil so that we can have eternal life with him in the Kingdom forever.

Even before a child is baptized, the priest must drive out or exorcize the evil from the child and from the baptismal water. Some people today may find these prayers' mention of evil, dark powers, the devil, and so forth, strange or unsettling. However, these prayers reflect the reality that even in our postmodern world, evil and darkness are quite real. Therefore, before entering into God's sacred community, we must be cleansed from the darkness that ensnares us. The reality of evil is made explicit in these exorcism prayers at the mention of the devil lurking in this world:

> The Lord puts you under ban, O Devil: he who came into the world, and made his abode among men, that he might overthrow your tyranny and deliver men, who also upon the Tree did triumph over the adverse powers, when the sun was darkened and the earth did quake, and the graves were opened, and the bodies of the saints arose: who also by death annihilated death, and overthrew him who exercised the dominion of death . . .[2]
>
> God, holy, awesome and glorious, who is unsearchable and inscrutable in all his works and might, has foreordained for you the penalty of eternal punishment, O Devil: the same through us, his unworthy servant, commands you, with all your hosts, to depart hence, from (him or her) who has been newly sealed in the Name of the Lord Jesus Christ, our true God. Wherefore I charge you, most crafty, impure, vile, loathsome, and alien spirit, by the might of Jesus Christ, who has all power both in heaven and on earth, who said unto the deaf and dumb demon, "Come out of the man, and in nowise enter a second time into him: Depart! Acknowledge the vainness of your might, which has not power even over swine . . .[3]
>
> O Lord of Sabaoth, the God of Israel, who heals every malady and every infirmity: Look upon thy servant prove (him/her) and search (him/her) and root out of (him/her) every operation of the Devil. Rebuke the unclean spirits and expel them and purify the works of they hands, and exerting thy trenchant might, speedily crush down Satan under (his/her) feet; and give (him/her) victory over the same.[4]

To many, this ancient rite of exorcism may seem out of touch with our modern understanding of human anthropology, which emphasizes solving problems and ignores concepts like evil, darkness, and sin. However, there is much to be said for reclaiming this theological vocabulary. These prayers, although very ancient, also help us

---

2. "First Prayer of Exorcism," in Paul Lazor, editor, *Baptism* (New York: Department of Religions Education, The Orthodox Church of America, 1994), 33–34.

3. "Second Prayer of Exorcism," 35–36.

4. "Third Prayer of Exorcism," 37–38.

to understand the pastoral nature of this important liturgical event. There is no doubt that after witnessing and praying the prayers of Baptism, one begins to understand the series of events that lead to the reception of Holy Communion. The sacrament of Baptism is a reminder of our life in Christ.

After reciting these three exorcism prayers, the priest then breathes upon the child three times, saying the following words, "Expel from (him/her) every evil and unclean spirit which hides and makes its lair in (his/her) heart."[5] The priest then asks the sponsors to renounce Satan and spit upon him while facing the West. This renunciation is not just a turning away, but a complete rejection of Satan and his hosts. We must first reject the devil and all his hosts before we can turn to Christ and confess him as King and God. The Apostle Paul goes a step further and states that we not only have to reject evil but actually fight against it; his epistle to the Ephesians is full of military imagery and metaphor that sometimes gets lost in preaching and proclamation.[6] Christians are still called to actively fight against the injustices of the world through the use of our spiritual weapons:

> Therefore, put on the armor of God, that you may be able to resist on the evil day and, having done everything, to hold your ground. So stand fast with your loins girded in truth, clothed with righteousness as a breastplate, and your feet shod in readiness for the gospel of peace. In all circumstances, hold faith as a shield, to quench all (the) flaming arrows of the evil one. And take the helmet of salvation and the sword of the Spirit, which is the word of God. (Eph 6:13–17)

These are not weapons of stealth or power, but weapons of peace that are in constant battle with the evil of this age. Paul lived in Roman society, where military metaphors would have been easily understood. Perhaps we would be better served if we reclaimed the forceful imagery of spiritual weapons. The Christian calling is a difficult one, and we fight for it in our daily lives. Our entire lives are is a battle between truth and falsehood, and between doing right and doing wrong. This battle begins at Baptism, and doesn't end until our last breath:

---

5. "Third Prayer of Exorcism," 37–38.

6. See Eph 6:10-20; see also Phil 1:27–30.

The first act of the Christian life is renunciation, a challenge. No one can be Christ's until he has, first, faced evil, and then become ready to fight it. How far is this spirit from the way in which we often proclaim, or to use a more modern term, "sell" Christianity today! Is it not usually presented as a comfort, help, release from tensions, a reasonable investment of time, energy and money? One has only to read—be it but once—the topics of the Sunday sermons announced in the Saturday newspapers, or the various syndicated "religious columns," to get the impression that "religion" is almost invariably presented as salvation of man and the world. How could we then speak of "fight" when the very setup of our churches must, by definition, convey the idea of softness, comfort, and peace? How can the Church use again the military language, which was its own in the first days, when it still thought of itself as *militia Christi*? One does not see very well where and how "fight" would fit into the weekly bulletin of a suburban parish, among all kinds of counseling sessions, bake sales, and "young adult" get-togethers.[7]

In the Eastern tradition, after the prayers of exorcism, the sponsors together with the child turn toward the East, toward Jerusalem, and toward the rising of the sun as they make a confession of faith. Three times the sponsors briefly turn toward the West, renounce Satan and his hosts, and then turn toward the East and confess Christ:

> The catechumen confesses his faith in Christ as King and as God. The two titles are not synonymous or repetitious. To believe in Christ as God is not sufficient, for the demons themselves believe in Him (Jas 2:19). To accept Him as King or Lord means precisely the desire and the decision to follow Him, to make one's whole life a service to Him, to live according to His commandments. This is why the earliest Christian confession of Christ was the confession and proclamation of Him as *Kyrios*, the Lord, a term which in religious and political language of that time implied the idea of an actual and total power demanding unconditional obedience. Christians were persecuted and put to death because they refused to address the title of "Lord" to the Roman Emperor.[8]

The catechumen or sponsor then makes a confession of faith, which is expressed through the recitation of the

---

7. Alexander Schmemann, *For the Life of the World* (Crestwood, NY: St. Vladimir's Seminary Press, 1979), 71.

8. Ibid., 34.

Nicene-Constantinopolitan Creed. The Creed is a synopsis or recapitulation of the story of our salvation, which ends with the hope of the Kingdom of God. The Creed is our statement of faith, our mission statement about what it means to live our calling as Christians. In sum, the Creed encapsulates our entire faith in Jesus Christ, in God the Father, and in the Holy Spirit. It also provides us with a way of life that—if we take it seriously—is the narrow way that the Lord speaks about in the Gospels. After the sponsors have rejected Satan and the darkness, the priest asks them three times, "Have you united yourself to Christ?" and they respond, "I have united myself to Christ."[9] The priest must make sure there is no doubt that the person is committed to what is about to take place; from this very moment, there is no turning back.

After the prayers of exorcism and the recitation of the Creed, the priest begins the Baptism proper. As with all liturgical services in the Orthodox Church the priest begins by reciting the Great Litany. During the rite of Baptism, the priest adds additional petitions for the child who has come to be baptized, and for the water in the baptismal font:

> That this water maybe sanctified with the power and effectual operation, and descent of the Holy Spirit, let us pray to the Lord.
>
> That there may be sent down into it the grace of redemption and the blessing of the Jordan, let us pray to the Lord.
>
> That we may be enlightened by the light of understanding and piety, and by the descent of the Holy Spirit, let us pray to the Lord.
>
> That (he/she) who is baptized therein may be made worthy of the kingdom incorruptible, let us pray to the Lord.
>
> That (he/she) may be a member and partaker of the death and resurrection of Christ our God, let us pray to the Lord.
>
> That (he/she) may preserve his/her Baptismal garment and the earnest of the Spirit pure and undefiled until the dread Day of Christ our God, let us pray to the Lord.[10]

Only after the Great Litany does the priest begin the great prayer over the baptismal water. Schmemann speaks of this prayer as a

---

9. "Third Prayer of Exorcism," 46–47.

10. Ibid.

kind of Eucharistic prayer, since it contains the elements of the
various anaphoras in the Eucharistic rite:

> It is a solemn act of praise and thanksgiving, an act of adoration by
> which man, on behalf of the whole world, responds to God. And this is
> the eucharist and adoration that takes us back to the beginning, makes
> us indeed witnesses of creation. For thanksgiving is truly the first and the
> essential act of man, the act by which he fulfills himself as man. The one
> who gives thanks is no longer a slave; there is no fear, no anxiety, no envy
> in adoration. Rendering thanks to God, one becomes free again, free in
> relation to God, free in relation to the world.[11]

The God who created the world and everything in it comes to
restore creation to what it was supposed to be from the very beginning. The great prayer of water blessing is very similar to the anaphora
prayers in the liturgy. They bring to mind all that God has done for
us, as we see in the following prayer for the water:

> For Thou, of Thine own good will, has brought all things into being
> which before were not, and by thy might though upholds creation, and by
> thy providence thou orders the world. When thou had joined together the
> universe out of four elements, Thou did crown the circle of the year with
> four seasons. Before Thee tremble all the powers endowed with intelligence.
> The sun sings unto Thee, the moon glorifies Thee. The stars meet together
> before Thy presence. The light obeys Thee. The deeps tremble before Thee.
> The water springs are subject unto Thee. Thou have spread out the heavens
> as if it were a curtain. Thou had established the earth upon the waters.
> Thou had set round about the sea barriers of sand. Thou had shed abroad
> the air for breathing. The angelic powers serve Thee. The choirs of
> Archangels fall down in adoration before Thee. The many-eyed Cherubim
> and the six winged Seraphim as they stand round about and fly, veil their
> faces in awe before Thine ineffable glory.[12]

Immediately following this prayer, the priest blesses the oil of the
catechumens for the traditional pre-baptismal anointing. Compared
with the other prayers in the Baptism service, the prayer over the oil is
rather short. In it we hear about Noah and the dove who brought back
the olive twig as a sign that the flood waters had dissipated. We are
also reminded that the oil delivers the gift of the Holy Spirit, which is

---

11. Schmemann, *Of Water and Spirit*, 46.
12. Ibid.

the fulfillment of Baptism. The priest asks the Lord to bless the oil so that it can be a protection against corruption and that it will be like an "armor of righteousness to the renewing of soul and body."[13] Before anointing the child with the oil, the priest drops oil into the font three times in the form of the cross, each time chanting "Alleluia," followed by a response ("Alleluia" three times) from the choir. "Alleluia" is the perfect prayer of praise, and it literally means *praise for the* LORD. Throughout the Old Testament, and especially in the Psalms, the phrase Alleluia appears quite frequently, as various authors praise Yahweh for his deliverance and protection from enemies. Thus as the priest blesses the oil and asks the Holy Spirit to come and sanctify the water, the community acknowledges God's sovereign power over the darkness and the evil of this world. Then the priest anoints the forehead, breast, shoulders, ears, hands, and feet of the child. We will see later that Schmemann connects this baptismal anointing with ordination; as we are anointed with holy oil in Baptism, we enter into the royal priesthood of all believers, which empowers us to offer praise and prayer to God.

Immediately following this prayer is a sort of epiclesis or calling down of the Holy Spirit upon the water, which does not merely make the water holy, but restores it to what it was supposed to be from the beginning. We are called to remember that the water is symbolic of the purification of sins, the illumination of soul and body, and the fountain of life. In other words, this great blessing of the water calls to remembrance all the great deeds that God has performed with water throughout time: drawing water from the rock in the desert,[14] saving Israel through the water of the Exodus,[15] and, of course, Jesus' own baptism in the Jordan River.[16] The epiclesis prayer is not to make the water holy or special but for us to again open our eyes and see what God has done for us through Jesus Christ:

> Following the great prayer of blessing the priest then takes the child and submerges him in the font three times, repeating the Trinitarian formula, "The child of God (name) is baptized in the Name of the Father, and of

---

13. Ibid.
14. See Ex 17:1–7.
15. See Ex 14.
16. See Mt 3:13–17; Mk 1:9–11; Lk 3:21–22; Jn 1:29–34.

the Son, and of the Holy Spirit. Amen." The child is then given a white garment as a sign of acceptance of this new life.[17]

The child has gone through the first rites of initiation.

Immediately following the Baptism, the priest blesses the white baptismal garment, which is referred to as the "robe of righteousness," and says, "The servant of God (name) is clothed in the robe of righteousness, in the name of the Father, and of the Son, and the Holy Spirit."[18] In the Book of Revelation, a white robe is given to the martyrs, those who have sacrificed their lives in obedience to the Lamb of God: "After this I had a vision of a great multitude, which no one could count, from every nation, race, people, and tongue. They stood before the throne and before the Lamb, wearing white robes and holding palm branches in their hands" (Rv 7:9). The martyrs are those who sacrificed their lives for the Gospel in times of persecution. They refused to reject Christ and worship Caesar, and thereby secured a place in the Kingdom. The Church has retained the symbolism of the white robe, in remembrance of the Death of Christ and as a reminder that Christians are called to be living witnesses to the Gospel, even if we are not physically put to death. After the blessing of the baptismal garment, sometimes the child is given a cross to wear as a sign of obedience and discipleship; this cross is not formally mentioned in the rubrics or texts of the baptismal service, yet it may provide another physical reminder that we are called to "clothe ourselves with Christ" and follow him.

While Baptism is the entrance into the Death and Resurrection of Christ, Chrismation (or Confirmation) is the gift of the Holy Spirit. Chrism, or *myron*, is a mixture of oil and various herbs that are simmered together on a stove for a long period of time. The oil is then bottled by the bishop and distributed to each of the parishes to be used by the priest for Chrismation. As in the Roman tradition, it is very symbolic that the bishop makes the chrism and then gives it to his priests. This shows unity with the bishop. In the Eastern tradition, Chrismation has always been closely connected with the rite of Baptism: Baptism provides entrance into the Church, and Chrismation seals or affirms that Baptism, which is finally fulfilled in the reception of Holy

---

17. Schmemann, *Of Water and Spirit*, 71.
18. Lazor, *Baptism*, 57.

Communion. The separation of the two rites that occurred in the Western Church never happened in the East. Kavanagh sees this separation as causing a theological confusion, allowing the meaning of the sacrament to shift from a sealing of baptismal graces to a mature faith commitment.

The neophyte is now a member of a community of faith, an *ecclesia* larger than himself or herself that includes a variety of persons, personalities, and gifts. The newly baptized person does not cease to be an individual, but becomes part of a new community, a community of the baptized. In the words of the Second Vatican Council's document *Lumen Gentium*: "In virtue of this catholicity each individual part contributes through its special gifts to the good of the other parts and of the whole Church. Through the common sharing of gifts and through the common effort to attain fullness in unity, the whole and each of the parts receive increase."[19]

The rite of Chrismation is brief in comparison to the numerous prayers that take place immediately prior to and during the Baptism. The rite of holy Chrismation has only one prayer, which the priest says before he anoints the child:

> Blessed art thou, O Lord almighty, Source of all good things, Sun of Righteousness, who sheds forth upon them that were in darkness the light of salvation, through the revelation of thine Only begotten Son and our God; and who has given unto us, unworthy though we may be, blessed purification through hallowed water, and divine sanctification through life-creating Chrismation; who now, also, has been graciously pleased to regenerate thy servant that has newly received illumination, by water and the Spirit, and grants unto (him/her) remission of sins, whether voluntary or involuntary. Do thou the same Master, compassionate King of kings, grant also unto (him/her) the seal of the gift of thy holy, and almighty, and adorable Spirit, and participation in the Body and precious blood of thy Christ. Keep (him/her) in thy sanctification, confirm (him/her) in the Orthodox faith; deliver (him/her) from the Evil One, and from all his workings. And preserve (his/her) soul in purity and righteousness, through the saving fear of thee, that (he/she) may please thee in every deed and word, and may be a child and heir of thy heavenly kingdom. For thou art our God, the God who shows mercy and who

---

19. Second Vatican Council, Dogmatic Constitution on the Church, *Lumen Gentium* (1964), 13.

saves, and unto thee do we ascribe glory, to the Father, and to the Son, and to the Holy Spirit now, and ever, and unto ages of ages. Amen.[20]

This prayer immediately seals the Baptism that took place moments before, and looks forward to the reception of Holy Communion, which fulfills them both. This prayer is the final affirmation of the child's new life in Christ; he or she is now receiving the gift of the Holy Spirit, whom the evangelist John calls the Counselor[21] and the Comforter.[22] The Holy Spirit descends upon the Apostles on the feast of Pentecost in tongues of fire, and sends them out into the world to proclaim the Gospel. Thus it is the Spirit who sanctifies, enlivens, and edifies. It is the Spirit of truth and unity who draws people together in the name of Christ.

In the act of Chrismation, the priest anoints the forehead, eyes, ears, chest, hands, and feet saying these words, "The seal of the gift of the Holy Spirit." The term "seal" is derived from the Greek work *sphragis*, which refers to a seal or brand. In antiquity, it was commonplace for a master to have the slaves of his household marked with a sign or seal, much like cattle are branded today. If the slaves ran away, they would be returned, since they bore the mark of the master. Likewise, official documents such as records or letters were sealed with a special stamp or seal in order to show from where the letter originated. Thus the neophytes are marked as belonging to the Holy Spirit just as they begin their new lives in Christ.

The prayer also speaks of the "gift of the Holy Spirit." The Holy Spirit himself is gift is given to us; but the Apostle Paul also speaks of the fruits of the Spirit, which can be likened to a gift: "love, joy, peace, patience, kindness, generosity, faithfulness, gentleness, self-control. Against such there is no law" (Gal 5:22–23). The newly-Chrismated Christian is branded with the Holy Spirit, the life-giver. Schmemann speaks of the sacrament of Chrismation as a gift, not only as a gift given to the Church as the conduit through which people enter the Church, but as a personal gift, a personal Pentecost for each of us:

---

20. "Third Prayer of Exorcism," 58.

21. Jn 14:16.

22. Jn 15:26.

And that we receive this personal gift of Christ's own Spirit not only because we are Christ's by faith and love, but because this faith and love have made us desire His life, to be in Him, and because in Baptism, having been baptized into Christ, we have been clothed with Christ. Christ is the Anointed and we receive his anointment; Christ is the Son and we are adopted as sons; Christ has the Spirit as His life in Himself and we are given participation in His life. And thus, in this unique, marvelous and truly divine anointment, the Holy Spirit, because He is the Spirit of Christ, gives Christ to us, and Christ, because the Holy Spirit is His Life, gives the Spirit to us: "The Spirit of truth, the gift of sonship, the pledge of future inheritance, the first fruits of eternal blessings, the life-creating power, the fountain of sanctification. . ."[23]; or, as another ancient liturgical formula says, "the grace of our Lord Jesus Christ, the love of God the Father, the communion of the Holy Spirit"—the gift and revelation of man to the Triune God Himself, the knowledge of Him, the communion as the Kingdom of God and life eternal.[24]

Following the work of Orthodox theologians Afanasiev and Evdokimov, Schmemann affirmed that in many ways the rite of Chrismation is akin to our ordination into the royal priesthood or priesthood of all believers:

Such is the gift of the Holy Spirit, the meaning of our personal Pentecost in the sacrament of the holy anointment. It seals, that is, makes, reveals, and confirms, us as members of the Church, the Body of Christ, as citizens of the Kingdom of God, as partakers of the Holy Spirit. And by this seal, it truly makes into ourselves, "ordains" each one of us to be and to become that which God from all eternity wants us to be, revealing our true personality and thus our only self-fulfillment.[25]

In his book *The Church of the Holy Spirit*, Afanasiev reviews the historical development of the rites of initiation, primarily Baptism and Chrismation, and compares them with the received rite of ordination.

---

23. *Divine Liturgy of St. John Chrysostom*, Prayer at the Anaphora, (South Canaan, PA: St. Tikhon's Seminary Press, 1977), 128.

24. Ibid.

25. In his collection of talks called *Liturgy and Life*, Schmemann remarks upon the sacrament of Baptism in the following way, "One could call it the ordination of a man to membership in the Church. In Baptism he received the new life and was introduced into the realm of the incarnation, of the new nature. Now, he has received his own unique personality, personal life, to be personally a living member of the body, a witness to Christ, a son of God, a partaker in the 'royal priesthood' of the Church" (97).

He reviews and compares both the prayers and the forms of each rite and concludes:

> This affinity is not coincidental. It bears witness to the fact that in liturgical consciousness, the sacrament of entrance into the Church was regarded as the sacrament of ordination for a newly baptized person. The historical sequence in which these elements of both sacraments emerged is not important. For me, however it is important to emphasize that liturgical thought deliberately puts these elements together and thus establishes a fundamental connection between both these sacraments. The newly baptized, spiritually born in the sacrament of Baptism, is ordained for the service in the Church, for carrying out his calling as a member of God's people, a nation of kings and priests so that they may keep "the garment of incorruption and the seal of the Spirit undefiled and unstrained in the fearful day of Christ our God." The Spirit is a pledge of a future age, a coming *aeon* of the Spirit which will come at the "day of the Lord." The one who preserves the "seal of the Spirit" will preserve himself on the day of the Lord which is coming in every Eucharist in which he serves God together with all the people.[26]

Afanasiev compares Baptism and ordination, and alludes to the parallel actions in both sacraments: the laying on of hands—of the priest in Baptism, and of the bishop in ordination—the giving of a white robe, the anointing with holy oil, and a tonsure of hair. In his book *Ages of the Spiritual Life,* Evdokimov also alludes to the similarity between the sacraments of Chrismation and ordination: "Before everything else, all are equal members of the People of God. By Baptism, 'the second birth,' all are already priests, and it is in the heart of this priestly equality that the functional differentiation of charisma is produced. It is not a new 'consecration' of a bishop or priest, but an ordination for a new ministry of one who was already consecrated, already changed in his nature once and for all, having already received his priestly character."[27]

Schmemann and others—such as Evdokimov and Afanasiev—compare the reception of holy chrism at Baptism to that at ordination, since in both sacraments, the gift of the Holy Spirit is given to the

---

26. Nicholas Afanasiev, *The Church of the Holy Spirit* (Notre Dame, IN: University of Notre Dame Press, 2007), 30.

27. Paul Evdokimov, *The Ages of Spiritual Life* (Crestwood, NY: St. Vladimir's Seminary Press, 1998), 200.

recipient. This baptismal "ordination" into the universal priesthood of all believers, also called the royal priesthood, is patterned after the life of Christ himself. Jesus is the messianic King who came to unite humanity to his divinity, who by grace makes us children of God. We know that Christ is not only King but also Prophet and Priest; by receiving Baptism and Chrismation, we enter into this kingly, prophetic, and priestly ministry of Christ. Through the grace of our baptismal calling to be followers of Christ, we are "'a chosen race, a royal priesthood, a holy nation, a people of his own, so that you may announce the praises' of him who called you out of darkness into his wonderful light. Once you were 'no people' but now you are God's people; you 'had not received mercy' but now you have received mercy" (1 Pt 2:9–10). In the words of God himself to Moses, "Therefore, if you hearken to my voice and keep my covenant, you shall be my special possession, dearer to me than all other people, though all the earth is mine. You shall be to me a kingdom of priests, a holy nation. That is what you must tell the Israelites" (Ex 19:6).

Schmemann's distinct theological contribution to this conversation connects the function of this universal priesthood to the Eucharistic liturgy, and ultimately to communion with Christ. It is within the ecclesial context that the universal priesthood is fulfilled and expressed. As Schmemann comments, the two forms of priestly ministry should be viewed as complementary, not in opposition to one another. There is distinction and differentiation of gifts between the two priesthoods, but their goal and focus is the same. Schmemann continues his comments on the universal priesthood by clarifying that "with this exclamation we are reminded that the meaning of the liturgy is not that in it the priest serves for the laity, or that the laity participates in the service each 'for himself,' but that the entire assembly, in the mutual submission of all ministries one to another, constitutes a single body for the realization of the priesthood of Jesus Christ."[28] A similar sentiment is expressed and expanded upon in an earlier chapter of *Liturgy and Life,* where Schmemann discusses the relationship between the universal and the institutional, or ordained, priesthood:

> The worshipping Church thus represents (makes present, actualizes) the whole Christ: the Head and the Body, the Divine and the Human, the Gift and its Acceptance; and the Orthodox Church, as expressed in

---

28. Ibid.

her liturgy, is neither clerical (the clergy being the only active element, and laity the passive one) nor egalitarian (which implies that there is a confusion between clergy and laity, both elements having equal right). In her teaching the harmony of all ministries—in their unity and in their distinction, in the active cooperation of all elements of the Church, under the guidance and the sanction of the hierarchy, in a cooperation which finds its pattern in worship—is essential for the spiritual welfare of the Church, its "fullness in Christ."[29]

Schmemann reflects upon the calling of the priesthood in the Church, and states that there is only one vocation in the Church:

> That vocation is to become a priest over creation, to offer prayers and spiritual sacrifices and to ultimately transform this world. But then the Church, who is the gift and the presence of this new life in the world, who therefore is offering, sacrifice, and communion, is also and of necessity priestly in her totality as the Body of Christ, and in her members as members of the body.[30]

It is this priesthood, which Adam lost in Eden, that we need to reclaim as ours. Adam refused to be the priest, to offer thanksgiving to God for everything, which led to utter denial of God and his life. Since Adam, humanity has always fallen short of our high calling to offer praise and prayer to God—that is, we have failed to fulfill our priestly vocation. Schmemann reminds us that our primary calling in life is to reclaim this priesthood for ourselves, and moreover, to foster a sense of gratitude in life. The theological vision of this priesthood is ultimately and fully expressed in the Eucharistic liturgy. The liturgical prayers, blessings, and hymns—the *ordo*, as Schmemann often calls it—reveal the organic and holistic nature of the royal priesthood. There can be no royal priesthood, no community, apart from the ordained priesthood, just as there can be no Body without the Head, Christ.

---

29. Schmemann, *Liturgy and Life*, 38.
30. Schmemann, *Of Water and the Spirit*, 97.

Chapter 6

Holy Orders and Clericalism

As we have seen, Schmemann argued quite forcefully for a strong Eucharistic ecclesiology, where both clergy and laity are fulfilling their roles in the royal priesthood and building up the Body of Christ, fed and nourished by the Word and the Eucharist and given the gifts and charisms of the Holy Spirit. Yet we know that things don't always work well, and very often, even in the Church, divisions occur. One of the biggest divisions that Schmemann addresses in his writings is clericalism, a problem not just in his time, but one that continues today.

Recent scholarship has argued that clericalism is one of the biggest pastoral problems plaguing both Eastern and Western Christians today.[1] Clericalism creates an ideological and theological separation among the people of God into two separate and seemingly unequal classes or castes: the clergy and the laity. While there are differences in the functions of the clergy and the laity, the dividing lines are sometimes overemphasized, creating a division or separation between the two. Schmemann found an answer to clericalism by looking once again at liturgical worship, specifically, the Eucharist. The liturgical language, blessings, prayers, processions, feasts and fasts, and hymnography remind us that the Church is the gathering of the entire Body of Christ—men and women, clergy and lay—around the Lord's altar.

Unfortunately, however, there are divisions within this body. Clericalism is a result of a reduction of ministry, where clergy live in physical, social, and spiritual isolation both from other members of the clergy and from the laity. This separation usually does not occur consciously, but is a result of many factors: isolation in seminary

---

1. For discussion on this topic, see George Wilson, SJ, *Clericalism: The Death of the Priesthood* (Collegeville, MN: Liturgical Press, 2008); and Geoffrey Robinson, *Confronting Power and Sex in the Catholic Church: Reclaiming the Spirit of Jesus* (Collegeville, MN: Liturgical Press, 2008).

formation, isolation in parish life, isolation in social and recreational activities. Schmemann had keen insight into this problem, having spent most of his adult life teaching, preaching, and being a pastor at a theological seminary, where he was constantly exposed to the many facets of ecclesial life, especially the problem of clericalism. He identified clericalism as a major roadblock that needed to be overcome in order to regain a sacramental worldview that is centered around the Eucharist. Schmemann envisioned a Church that was dynamic, robust, and vivified by the bread and wine of the Eucharistic Divine Liturgy: where priest and parishioner gathered around the same altar, recited the same prayers, and replied "Amen" together.

UNDERSTANDING CLERICALISM

In a small booklet titled *Clergy and Laity in the Orthodox Church*, published in 1952, Schmemann tried to address the problems of clericalism in the Church.[2] He prefaced his discussion by observing the vast misunderstandings, frustrations, and confusion regarding the relationship between clergy and laity. In his usual fashion, Schmemann revealed his pastoral acumen in explaining and interpreting such a multi-faceted issue.

He began the essay by providing definitions of clergy and laity, noting that these words have traditionally been defined in opposition to one another. He observed that even Webster's Dictionary defines laity as distinct from a professionalized clergy, who are the "body of men ordained to the service of God."[3] Schmemann states that these definitions themselves reveal a clear opposition regarding roles and functions within the Church, "They imply, also, in the case of laity, a negation. A layman is someone who has no particular status, not of a particular profession."[4] Having outlined the basic linguistic tensions between clergy and laity, Schmemann sets out to describe each group before he proposes a solution to the problem.

---

2. Alexander Schmemann, *Clergy and the Laity in the Orthodox Church* (Crestwood, NY: St. Vladimir's Seminary Press, 1952), 5. This short document was written in response to the anti-clerical attitude within the Russian Orthodox Metropolia (which later became the Orthodox Church of America) during the 1950s.

3. Ibid.

4. Ibid., 6.

Stating that the term "laity" is derived from the Greek word "*laos*," which refers to the "people of God," Schmemann extends this connection to the beloved "people of God" in the Scriptures, with whom God entered into the covenant. In the Old Testament, the "*laos*" referred to Israel, God's chosen people, while the New Testament writings include everyone who believes in God and his Son Jesus Christ. This leads Schmemann to say, "Thus, the Church, the community of those who believe in Christ, becomes the true people of God, the *laos*, and each Christian a *laikos*—a member of the People of God." Therefore the term *laos* "implies the ideas of full, responsible, active membership."[5]

Schmemann also reminds his readers that through the sacraments of Baptism and Chrismation, all Christians have been given the gifts of the Holy Spirit and have the power to use them for the common well-being of the Church—a theme that was explored in the previous chapter of this book. Schmemann also notes that these gifts, which allow the full participation of the laity in the Church, are clearly enumerated in the baptismal service of the Orthodox Church, which asks that the newly baptized person be ". . . an honorable member of God's Church, a consecrated vessel, a child of light, an heir of God's kingdom."[6] Quoting the Apostle Paul, Schmemann calls the laity "fellow citizens with the holy ones and members of the household of God" (Eph 2:19).

Schmemann goes on to emphasize that the liturgical prayers reflect the common ministry of the clergy and the laity. He reminds us that the prayers are written in the plural, which reflects the common work of the clergy and laity during the liturgical celebration: "*we* offer, *we* pray, *we* thank, *we* adore, *we* enter, *we* ascend, *we* receive."[7] Although there are a few prayers in the liturgies of St. John Chrysostom and St. Basil the Great that are specifically for the priest, even these are within the larger context of the communal gathering, and the emphasis remains on the entire worshipping community.

However, Schmemann notes that the liturgy reveals the *locus classicus* for the role of the laity: the laity, together with the clergy, celebrate the liturgy. In making his argument, Schmemann discusses

5. Ibid.

6. Ibid.

7. Ibid., italics in original.

the recitation of the common liturgical word "amen," which is used as a common response in the liturgy. Amen literally means "let it be" or "so be it;" the laity's role of affirmation in liturgy is indeed essential: "And 'amen' is indeed the word of the laity in the Church, expressing the function of the laity as the People of God, which freely and joyfully accepts the Divine offer, seals it with its consent. There is really no service and no liturgy, without the Amen of those who have been ordained to serve God as community, as Church."[8] The word "amen" is a sign that the entire ecclesial community is responsible for the common prayer of the Church, that both clergy and laity offer the one prayer to God in behalf of all and for all.

When Schmemann speaks of the common work and prayer of the laity, he is referring to the liturgical practice of concelebration. Schmemann says that the laity actually concelebrate with the clergy during the Divine Liturgy. Generally, in both East and West, the term "concelebration" usually refers to the liturgical practice of more than one priest celebrating the Divine Liturgy or Mass together. They are said to be concelebrants. In general use, this term refers specifically to the clergy.[9] However, Schmemann states that everyone gathered together during the Divine Liturgy, both clergy and laity, are offering the same prayer, the same blessing, the same offering, and the same thanksgiving; thus everyone concelebrates, with the celebrating priest. Schmemann then says, "Who is serving, in other words, is not the clergy, and not even the clergy with the laity, but the Church, which is constituted and made manifest in all fullness by everyone together."[10]

Schmemann's comments regarding the understanding of the term concelebration can be traced back to his mentor and teacher Nicholas Afanasiev, who proposed that the term "concelebration" refers to the entire gathering of the assembly and includes both clergy and laity: "everyone ministers to God at the Eucharist. Neither

---

8. Ibid. The same can be said of the Greek expression "axios" literally, "he is worthy," which is publicly pronounced at the rite of the ordination of a candidate to the diaconate or the presbyterate. The clergy and laity together shout "axios" at the appointed time during an ordination liturgy.

9. See "Ex Oriente Lux? Some Reflections on Eucharistic Concelebration," in Robert F. Taft, sj, *Beyond East and West: Problems in Liturgical Understanding*, 2nd ed. (Rome: Pontificio Instituto Orientale, 2001), 111–132.

10. Schmemann, *Clergy and the Laity in the Orthodox Church*, 88.

separate groups nor separate members celebrate: it is the Church that celebrates. Everyone concelebrates at the celebration of the one—their president. There can be no celebration of all and there can be no Eucharistic gathering apart from the one president."[11] Both Schmemann and Afanasiev emphasized that it is everyone's vocation to pray, to worship, to give thanks, to offer, and to bless. Therefore the entire Church concelebrates around the one bread and the one cup on the one altar. Thus the entire Church, clergy and laity together, offer their common worship to God as everyone participates in the liturgical services.

While it is true that everyone offers the common prayer, blessing, and offering, there are still distinctions between the clergy and the laity. While everyone is a member of the *laos,* the people of God, not everyone is a member of the clergy. The term clergy, derived from the Greek term *kleros,* designates those whom God has set apart for service or duty. The clergy in the East and West are thus the deacons, priests, and bishops who have been ordained for a specific service within the larger Church structure. The members of the clergy are neither "above the laity," nor are they entitled to special "rights;" rather, they live the same life of the Gospel, and work from within the same Church as those who are not ordained. Schmemann emphasized that the term *kleros* is very similar to the word *laos* and that "the clergy" means "that part of mankind that belongs to God, has accepted His call, has dedicated itself to God. In its initial meaning the whole Church is described as 'clergy'—part or inheritance."[12]

Clerical power is a great temptation. In numerous journal entries Schmemann reflected on the temptations to power and control in seminary life. In his journal entry from February 2, 1982, one year before his death, Schmemann wrote:

> Clericalism suffocates; it makes part of itself into the whole sacred character of the Church; it makes its power a sacred power to control, to lead, to administer, a power to perform sacraments, and in general, it makes any power a "power given to me." Clericalism separates all "sacredness" from the lay people: the iconostasis, communion (only by permission), theology. In short, clericalism is *de facto* denial of the Church as the Body

---

11. "The Lord's Supper," in Nicholas Afanasiev, Alvian Smirensky, trans., *The Limits of the Church*, Vitaly Permiakov, et al., trans., Michael Plekon, ed. Unpublished manuscript. The term "president" is synonymous with the term priest or presbyter.

12. Schmemann, *Clergy and Laity in the Orthodox Church*, 11.

of Christ, for in the body, all organs are related and different only in their functions, but not in their essence. And the more clericalism "clericalizes" (the traditional image of the bishop or the priest—emphasized by his clothes, hair, e.g., the bishop in full regalia!), the more the Church itself becomes more worldly, spiritually submits itself to this world. In the New Testament, the priest is presented as an ideal layman. But almost immediately there begins his increasingly radical separation from lay people, and not only separation, but opposition to lay people, contrast to them.[13]

This passage reveals Schmemann's understanding of the great temptations that power and authority are in the Church. Likewise, he sees the continued piety of the clergy as reinforcing this separation, which consequently continues to alienate the laity. This vision of authority is contrary to that which is given to us in both the Scriptures and tradition. Throughout the Gospel, Jesus teaches his disciples about serving others as the supreme act of love, especially as he himself washes the feet of his disciples, telling them that if they want to follow him they must wash one another's feet.

Schmemann also laments the fact that some seminaries seem to foster clericalism by admitting students who seek power and control. In another journal entry Schmemann remarks:

The tragedy of theological education lies in the fact that young people who seek priesthood are—consciously or unconsciously—seeking this separation, power, this rising above the laity. Their thirst is strengthened and generated by the whole system of theological education, of clericalism. How can they be made to understand, not only with their minds, but their whole being, that one must run away from power, any power, that it is always a temptation, always from the devil? Christ freed us from that power—"All authority in heaven and on earth has been given to me . . ." (Mt 28:18)—by revealing the Light of power as power of love, of sacrificial self-offering. Christ gave the Church not "power," but the Holy Spirit: "receive the Holy Spirit . . ." In Christ, power returned to God, and man was cured from ruling and commanding.[14]

On another day, he writes:

---

13. Schmemann, *Journals*, 310.
14. Ibid., 311.

In the sixty-first year of my life, I suddenly ask myself: How has it all become so perverted? And I become afraid![15]

His comments may sound like a gross generalization, and perhaps they are. He wrote that first journal entry one year before his death, after more than thirty years of teaching in Orthodox theological seminaries, both in North America and in Europe. His many years in formal seminary education and pastoral formation were the fertile ground that gave rise to his insights about the detriments of clericalism. Whatever inspired Schmemann to write such words must have caused him great grief and concern. It is important to note that many seminarians turn out to be excellent deacons, priests, and bishops, as well as lay leaders in the Church. Many go on for further education and training; some may return to a seminary or Church institution as a professor, instructor, or administrator. Still others are involved in missionary work, outreach programs, and so forth. Seminaries in both East and West have produced some very dedicated and devout men whose hearts are in the right place and who have a zeal for serving others. However, it is important—if not essential—for us to keep in mind the temptations toward clerical power and authority over the laity.

This misunderstanding of the roles and functions of clergy and laity was clear to Schmemann. He was raised in a clerical Orthodox Church in Europe and found a similar situation in the United States. Some of the problems and issues involved clergy-lay relations, and trying to find an answer to problems of rights, duties, and obligations of the priest and the parishioners.

Schmemann also warned of the opposite problem. In congregationalism, the laity take ecclesial life into their own hands, so to speak, and reduce the role of the priest to that of a liturgical servant. The Church has suffered from a strong congregationalism at various times, notably the Roman Catholic Church in the American Colonial period, when there were few clergy to serve the needs of the growing Catholic Church in North America. The Orthodox Church had similar problems during the times of the Great Immigration from Europe, most prominently in the early years of the 20th century. Because of their presence in society, American laity often attempt to insert the American ideals of liberty, democracy, rights, and duties

15. Ibid., 231.

into the Church. Others may seek to become little priests by trying to gain some of the sacramental power and authority of the clergy through an abundance of "lay ministries," which are somehow supposed to be different from "clerical ministry."[16] Schmemann refuted both visions. Toward the end of his essay on clerical and lay relations, he wrote:

> The conclusion is clear: there is no opposition between clergy and laity in the Church. Both are essential. The Church as a totality is Laity and the Church as a totality is the inheritance of God, the Clergy of God. And in order to be this, there must exist within the Church the distinction of functions, of ministries that complete one another. The clergy are ordained to make the Church the gift of God—the manifestation and communication of His truth, grace and salvation to men. It is their sacred function, and they fulfill it only in complete obedience to God. The laity are ordained to make the Church the acceptance of that gift, the "Amen" of mankind to God. They equally can fulfill their function only in complete obedience to God. It is the same obedience: to God and to the Church that establishes the harmony between clergy and laity, make them one body, growing into the fullness of Christ.[17]

Schmemann contrasted the power and authority that clergy may seek with the real power of Jesus. Jesus became powerful in his weakness and humility, which were manifested in his Death on the cross. It is in this self-sacrifice and spirit of humility that the Christian is powerful. Jesus' image of a servant leader was one who washes the feet of his disciples; as he commands Peter: "I have given you a model to follow, so that as I have done for you, you should also do."[18]

CLERGY AND LAITY WORKING TOGETHER

Schmemann's unique contribution to the understanding of pastoral theology and ministry is based on the conciliar nature of the Church, which is a hallmark of the Eastern Christian theological tradition. This understanding of the Church as council—often referred to as the Church's *sobornal* nature—was a model of the Church highlighted by

---

16. Ibid., 329.
17. Ibid., 13.
18. See Jn 13:15.

the Paris School theologians in the early 20th century.[19] While these theologians wrote on various and diverse topics, one common theme runs throughout their writings: the Church is not composed just of a clergy who are apart from the rest of the people, nor is it a congregationalist group of laity only, but the entire people of God, clergy and laity gathered together at the one altar offering their prayers and praise to God, united in the Eucharist. This theme of the conciliar nature of the Church, also called Eucharistic ecclesiology, can be seen throughout the writings of the Paris School theologians, both in the Eastern Church—Paul Evdokimov, Nicolas Afanasiev, Sergei Bulgakov—and in the Western Church—Yves Congar, Jean Daniélou, Henri de Lubac. Each of these scholars had a deep impact on Schmemann's theological vision of the Church; therefore it is no accident that their understanding of the Church as council would be a prevalent theme in his own writings as well.

Once again Schmemann returns to the sacramental understanding of the Church: that it is the Eucharist that unites all of us together in the one bread and the one cup, and thus also unites the earthly and the heavenly. "The institution is sacramental because its whole purpose is constantly to transcend itself as an institution, to fulfill and actualize itself as the New Being; and it can be sacramental because as institution it corresponds to the reality it fulfills, is its real image."[20] This sacramental aspect of the community underlies his approach to an overt clericalism. The priest is not reduced to the person who dispenses grace, but is one who unites a congregation in the one Eucharistic offering to Christ.

A sacramental image of the Church mirrors the Trinity; just as the Trinity is a council of three persons, Father, Son, and Spirit, who exist in the outpouring of their love, so too should the Church mimic or express itself as a council. Just as the Trinity is bound together in love, so are the clergy bound to the whole Church: they cannot be outside or apart from their congregations, but are within it.

---

19. Regarding the term *sobornost*: "In modern Russian theology it denotes a unity of persons within the organic fellowship of the Church, each person maintaining his full freedom and personal integrity." Elizabeth A. Livingstone, in *Concise Oxford Dictionary of the Christian Church* (New York: Oxford University, 1977), 470, cited in J. M. R. Tillard, *Flesh of the Church, Flesh of Christ: A Source of Eucharistic Communion* (Collegeville, MN: Pueblo Books, 2001), 62 n. 55.

20. Alexander Schmemann, "Toward a Theology of Councils," *St. Vladimir's Theological Quarterly* 6 no. 4 (1962): 163.

Similarly, just as the Trinity contains a hierarchy of persons, so do the various members of the Church have different functions. In a lengthy passage worth citing, Schmemann outlines the hierarchical nature of the Trinity in terms of the rest of the members of the Body of Christ, especially those in ministry:

> Whatever is truly conciliar is truly personal and, therefore, truly hierarchical. And the Church is hierarchical simply because she is the restored life, the perfect society, the true council. To ordain someone to a hierarchical function does not mean his elevation "above" the others, his opposition to them as "power" and "submission." It means the recognition by the Church of his personal vocation within the ecclesia, of his appointment by God, who knows the hearts of men and is, therefore, the source of all vocations and gifts. It is, thus, a truly conciliar act, for it reveals the obedience of all: the obedience of the one who is ordained, the obedience of those who ordain him, i.e., recognize in him the divine call to the ministry of government, the obedience of the whole Church to the will of God.[21]

The Church maintains a hierarchical structure, however, as Schmemann rightly states, it is not a hierarchy of power but an ordered structure.[22] According to the conciliar model, the Church is a community of the baptized saints who work together to build up the Body of Christ one person at a time through the exercise of the various of gifts and charisms that are distributed to each by the outpouring of the Holy Spirit. The Body only exists because it is Christ's Body, and it is held together by a continual outpouring of love.

Schmemann's best and most overlooked writing on the topic is a short essay called "Toward a Theology of the Council," in which he offers some very powerful and stimulating commentary on ministry in relation to the larger Church. It is a prophetic piece of writing, identifying clericalism and authority as two sources of temptation for clergy, and calling into question the typical relationship between bishop and priest, as well as the relationships between parish, diocese, and the universal Church.

---

21. Schmemann, "Toward a Theology of Councils," 166.

22. For a good survey of this topic of "ordered structure" see Susan K. Wood, ed., *Ordering the Baptismal Priesthood: Theologies of Lay and Ordained Ministry* (Collegeville, MN: Liturgical Press, 2003).

We cannot reduce the Church to its institutional aspects like church governance or administration, or what I like to call the everyday aspects of the Church: those small, seemingly mundane activities such as bulletins, phone calls, newsletters, meetings, and committees, which seem to overwhelm at times, especially in larger congregations.[23] Like Schmemann, we ought to see these everyday activities in an eschatological light, looking instead to the *Parousia* and our participation in that heavenly Kingdom that his Second Coming will inaugurate. Schmemann refuses to make a distinction between the human and heavenly nature of the Church—between what the sociologist of religions Mircea Eliade called the sacred and the profane.[24] Even the seemingly profane or mundane aspects of ecclesial life, which pastors know all too well, are important and have their rightful place in the larger scheme of things; all things, even parish council meetings, can be sanctified and redeemed by Christ through the cross and renewed and enlivened in the Eucharist. In this, Schmemann returns once again to the sacramental understanding of the Church, that it is the Eucharist that unites all of us together in the one bread and one cup, and thus also unites the earthly and the heavenly: "The institution is sacramental because its whole purpose is constantly to transcend itself as an institution, to fulfill and actualize itself as the New Being; and it can be sacramental because as institution it corresponds to the reality it fulfills, is its real image."[25] It is this sacramental aspect of the community that underlies his approach to pastoral theology. The priest is not merely the person who dispenses grace, but is the one who unites a congregation in the one Eucharistic offering to Christ, who sits on the throne with his Father.

These reflections make it quite clear that there is no place for clericalism or a top-down authority structure in a conciliar Church. Jesus came to serve the poor, the needy, those whom he called the least in this world, yet some clergy expect to be served rather than be the chief servants in the Church. The priest is called to be the exemplar of Christ to the community; though he is just as fallen and sinful

---

23. For some reflections on the day-to day activities of parish life see Allan Hugh Cole, Jr., Editor, *Midterms to Ministry: Practical Theologians on Pastoral Beginnings* (Grand Rapids, MI: Eerdmans, 2008).

24. Mircea Eliade, *The Sacred and the Profane: The Nature of Religion*, trans. Willard R. Trask (San Diego, Harcourt: 1987).

25. Alexander Schmemann, "Towards a Theology of Councils," 163.

as the all rest, he is the primary one to whom people go for counsel, advice, prayer, comfort, and encouragement. However, his words may not convey much of Christ if he considers himself of a separate, higher class than his parishioners.

At the opposite extreme, the Church cannot be reduced to a congregationalism that is reflective of the democratic society in which today's Church exists. In a congregationalist approach, the parish church is under the direct leadership of the local lay leaders, who hire and fire at will. The laity have direct authority over the funds and operating procedures of the local parish. The pastor may be the spiritual leader of the community in some abstract sense, but he serves—or leaves—according to the whims of the parish council.

Consideration of the Church's conciliar nature, which leads us to the Eucharistic table, provides a refreshing model that offers a solution to the problem of clericalism and the consequent issues of power and authority. There is no room for bickering, fighting, power, or authority to be exerted by anyone, yet there is still order and structure within the Body. The Body exists only because it is Christ's Body, and it is held together by a continual outpouring of love.

We have outlined Schmemann's understanding and explanation of clericalism and congregationalism as dividing the Church and causing great harm to pastoral theology. Both clericalism and congregationalism effect a false idea of the role of the laity, in comparison to that of the clergy. These two reductions provide the backdrop for Schmemann's critique of the Orthodox Church in the West, especially in the United States of America.

Chapter 7

The Liturgical Rite of Ordination

As Schmemann often mentions in his writings, when one looks at the sacraments of the Church—such as Baptism, marriage, Eucharist, and Holy Orders—one can better understand the meaning of the sacrament through the very prayers, hymns, and actions of the sacrament itself. In other words, the sacrament symbolically reveals its very meaning through its celebration. Therefore, as we look to Schmemann for his thoughts on pastoral theology, we must take a brief look at his commentary on the liturgical rite of priestly ordination, since it is in this sacrament that we see a fulfillment of Baptism. This is not a historical overview of the development of the rite of ordination, as Schmemann himself does not delve into this. However, his commentary provides us with great insight into his understanding of the meaning of ordination for the life of the Church and for the building up of the Body of Christ.[1]

Schmemann does not view the priest as having any special personal power or authority in the Church, but rather, deriving his authority from Christ himself. The ministry of the priest is to make Christ present to the community, primarily through the offering of the Eucharist. However, this sacramental ministry is done within the context of the Church community. Schmemann links the ordained priest with the Church in and through the sacraments. As there is no priesthood apart from Baptism, so too is there no priesthood apart from the Eucharist. It is customary for every priest to be ordained for a specific Eucharistic community; in other words, a priest is not a free

---

1. For a thorough analysis of the various rites of ordination see Paul F. Bradshaw, *Ordination Rites of the Ancient Churches of East and West* (Collegeville, MN: Pueblo, 1990).

agent but is always attached to a particular eparchy, diocese, or monastery. This communal understanding of the priesthood is expressed in the liturgy itself: a priest of the Eastern Church cannot celebrate a private Eucharist by himself, but must have at least one other person in attendance, thus expressing the true community of faith: clergy and laity worshipping together.[2]

Priestly ordinations take place immediately following the Great Entrance (in the Eastern Orthodox tradition), when the gifts of bread and wine are brought to the presiding bishop, who then puts the gifts on the altar table. Then two deacons bring the candidate for ordination through the royal doors, the two main doors located in the center of the icon screen [*iconostasis*], which are the doors through which the priest enters and exits during the course of the Liturgy. The two sub-deacons shout out the word "command" two times as the priestly candidate makes a full prostration to the ground—bowing toward the altar area. The third time, the deacons exclaim, "Command, most holy master." The fact that the ordination takes place during the course of the Divine Liturgy and that the deacons together with the entire congregation witness the ordination shows us that ordination is not done in private but is a communal act, revealing the communal nature of the Church. Then the candidate is escorted through the Royal Doors, where he is greeted by the concelebrating clergy. The royal doors as well as the two deacon's doors, the two doors on either side of the icon screen or *iconostasis*, remain open during the ordination, yet another way of expressing that the ordination is a public act. These doors are generally closed during the liturgical services except when the deacon or priest make their entrances or exits through the course of the Divine Liturgy. However, during the ordination service they are open. The candidate is then brought around the altar table three times in a counterclockwise procession, each time kissing the four corners of the altar table, since it is the same altar on which the young man will serve the holy Eucharist and offer prayers for the community. During this procession around the altar, the concelebrating clergy and the choir sing the following hymns:

---

2. The Roman Catholic Church likewise states that "Mass should not be celebrated without an assisting minister, or at least one of the faithful, except for a just and reasonable cause." (*General Instruction of the Roman Missal*, 254).

O holy martyrs, who fought the good fight and have received your crowns: entreat ye the Lord that our souls may be saved.

Glory to thee O Christ God, the Apostles' boast, the martyrs' joy, whose preaching was the consubstantial Trinity.

Rejoice O Isaiah! A virgin is with child, and shall bear a son, Emmanuel, both God and Man; and Orient is his name; whom magnifying we call the Virgin blessed.[3]

Interestingly, these hymns are the same ones that are also sung during the service of Holy Matrimony, but in the reverse order.[4] Schmemann notes this close connection between this part of the ordination service and the marriage service: "This is why the sacrament of ordination is, in a sense, identical with the sacrament of Matrimony. Both are manifestations of love. The priest is indeed married to the Church. But just as the human marriage is taken into the mystery of Christ and the Church and becomes the sacrament of the Kingdom, it is this marriage of the priest with the Church that makes him really priest, the true minister of love which alone transforms the world and reveals the Church as the immaculate bride of Christ."[5]

Then, with the laying on of hands, the ordaining bishop recites two short prayers:

O God, who has no beginning and no ending; who art older than every created thing; who crowns with the name of Presbyter those whom thou deems worthy to serve the word of thy truth in the divine ministry of this degree: Do thou, the same Lord of all men, deign to preserve in pureness of life and in unswerving faith this man also, upon whom, through me, thou has graciously been pleased to lay hands. Be favourably pleased to grant unto him the great grace of the Holy Spirit, and make him wholly thy servant in all things acceptable unto thee, and worthily exercising the great honours of the priesthood which thou has conferred upon him by thy prescient power . . .

---

3. Hapgood, *Service Book of the Holy Orthodox-Catholic Apostolic Church*, 316.

4. During the marriage service these hymns are chanted as the newly married couple makes a procession around the icon in the center of the Church, led by the priest who carries a hand cross. This is their first procession together as a couple, and it is a reminder that they are called to walk together behind Christ, following him in their marriage.

5. Schmemann, *For the Life of the World: Sacraments and Orthodox,* Second Expanded Edition (Crestwood NJ: St. Vladimir's Seminary Press, 1997), 94. It is debatable whether Schmemann is correct in his interpretation of the ordination service *vis à vis* the marriage service. More research has to be done on this connection.

O God great in might and inscrutable wisdom, marvelous in counsel above the sons of men: Do thou, the same Lord, fill with the gift of thy Holy Spirit this man whom it has pleased to thee to advance to the degree of Priest; that he may be worthy to stand in innocence before thine Altar; to proclaim the Gospel of thy kingdom, to minister the word of thy truth, to offer unto thee spiritual gifts and sacrifices; to renew thy people through the laver of regeneration. That when he shall go to meet thee, at the Second Coming of our great God and Savior, Jesus Christ, thine Only Begotten Son, he may receive the reward of a good steward in the degree committed unto him, through the plenitude of thy goodness.[6]

One might expect the ordination rite to be longer, but it only contains these two rather short prayers. Three times these prayers highlight the new priest's calling to be a servant of the Word; this emphasis on the preaching and teaching ministry of the priesthood is likewise noted in the service of the Divine Liturgy as the priest proclaims the sermon to the worshipping community. The other emphases in these two prayers commit the priest to offer spiritual sacrifices on behalf of the people and to perform Baptisms ("the laver of regeneration").

After the ordination itself, as the bishop is vesting the new priest, the congregation responds with the word "*Axios*," which is always recited in the original Greek. The word *axios* means "worthy," and all ordinations must include this affirmation by the congregation. The bishop, the concelebrating clergy, and the congregation all say "*axios*"; in other words, the congregation too must give their public acknowledgement that this person is indeed worthy to be a priest in the Church of God. Thus the priest's authority in the Church is not an authority apart from or above the congregation, but comes in part from within the congregation itself. It is the Church, the entire people of God, who give their "Amen," so to speak, to the priestly candidate.

The prayers are clear: the vocation of the priest is to lead the congregation in prayer, which is done primarily through the Eucharistic service, the Divine Liturgy; to proclaim the Gospel of truth and to teach it whenever possible; and to further the Gospel through the rite of Baptism. This list is not meant to exclude other responsibilities—both sacramental, such as Chrismation and burial,

---

6. Hapgood, *Service Book of the Holy Orthodox-Catholic Apostolic Church*, 316–317.

and practical, such as meetings and administrative tasks—so much as to highlight the most important.

Schmemann strongly argues that there is no special or unique vocation of the priesthood other than to reveal to others the common vocation of the entire people of God: to always offer thanksgiving to God. He was adamant that any theological or doctrinal separation between the vocations of the clergy and the laity is a false one, which reduces the priesthood to a separate caste of people, much like the Levites in the Old Testament, and thereby encourages clericalism.[7] According to Schmemann, "If there are priests in the Church, if there is the priestly vocation in it, it is precisely in order to reveal to each vocation its priestly essence, to make the whole life of all the liturgy of the Kingdom, to reveal the Church as the royal priesthood of the redeemed world. It is, in other terms, not a vocation 'apart,' but the expression of the love for man's vocation as the son of God and for the world as the sacrament of the Kingdom."[8] Thus the priest fulfills the calling of everyone who is a member of the royal priesthood, to offer our prayer and praise to God and to become fully a priest over creation, always giving thanks for everything.

Vocation to the Priesthood

However, in addition to this common vocation of the entire Church, Schmemann does acknowledge a specific and unique vocation to the priesthood. Ordination is not the beginning of one's vocation in the Church, but a fulfillment of his Baptism and Chrismation. Because of this, ordination requires preparation. Schmemann identifies three important areas of preparation for the priesthood: spiritual, intellectual, and practical.

Spiritual Preparation

Schmemann begins by stating that there is no specific spiritual preparation that is unique to the priesthood, because all Christians

---

7. This theme of clericalism is highlighted in an excellent essay by Kyprian Kern "Two Models of the Pastorate Levitical and Prophetic" in Michael Plekon, ed., *Tradition Alive: On the Church and the Christian Life in Our Time—Readings from the Eastern Church* (Lanham, MD: Rowman and Littlefield, 2003).

8. Schmemann, *For the Life of the World*, 93.

must be spiritual. Here, Schmemann rejects the "double ethical" spirituality approach for clergy and laity. Rather, all Christians must "become what they are: children of light, children of the kingdom."[9] The priest may be tempted to act as different and separate from the laity, but Schmemann reminds his readers that this is a false temptation, one that must be avoided at all costs:

> Paradoxical as it may seem, the root and the foundation of the spiritual preparation for priesthood is to take seriously Christian life as such and not the specifically "priestly life." It is indeed a strange yet common fact that this idea of a different and special priestly spirituality leads to a real atrophy of the common moral consciousness. We shall condemn gossip from the ambo but since our own "clerical gossip" is always rooted in one supposed zeal for the Church we shall practice it with delight—and, in fact, nowhere is there so much gossip, mutual criticism, suspicion and factionalism as in the clerical milieu. We shall warn our people that they must prepare themselves for communion by fasting and prayer, but since we ourselves receive it so often, we will easily dispense with such preparation. We shall constantly call the people to be generous and to give, yet having "given our whole life" to the Church we will think it perfectly rational for us to receive, but not to give . . . A first year seminarian has already a tendency to think that he is to learn to acquire something "specifically priestly," a way to walk and to speak, a way to behave which will make him "soon like a priest," and this feeling of belonging to a different and superior "caste" may obscure in him the very simple idea that to be a priest one must first of all, be a Christian—in the full meaning of this word. And to be a Christian, means, above everything else, to take seriously, directly and literally the commandments of Christ and to live by them.[10]

Schmemann begins his discussion of the ordained priesthood by speaking about what is asked of all Christians as stated by Jesus: "So be perfect, just as your heavenly Father is perfect" (Mt 5:48). Likewise, Schmemann regards the spiritual life not as something separate from daily existence, but something that organically flows from within: "In short, spiritual preparation of future priests consists in deepening by all possible means the Christian faith and life, in

---

9. Alexander Schmemann, "Notes on Pastoral Theology," Unpublished Alexander Schmemann Collection, Fr. Georges Florovsky Library, St. Vladimir's Orthodox Theological Seminary, Crestwood, NY, 5.

10. Ibid.

making religion not something added to life—as it is understood in our nominally Christian societies—but as life itself."[11]

Intellectual Preparation

When speaking about spiritual preparation for the priesthood, Schmemann also emphasizes the need for intellectual training and preparation for the priesthood. The candidate should read and pray the Scriptures, regularly attend worship, and practice the basic tenants of the Gospel: love, mercy, peace, forgiveness, humility, and generosity. Schmemann was adamant that the priest must have a well-rounded theological education. He often fought against minimalism in the Church, especially in theological training. Since the priest is the main liturgical celebrant, as well as the primary teacher and preacher, he needs to be well versed in the doctrines of the faith, and needs to know intimately the Christian faith and teachings.[12]

Schmemann also contends that, since we work out our salvation in a specific culture and society, the priestly candidate should be well versed in contemporary ethical, moral, and political struggles and temptations, so that he can adequately address these issues and concerns in his sermons and other teachings. Schmemann points out that in the age of the ecumenical councils, even the great theologians such as Basil the Great and John Chrysostom were aware of the culture and society around them. The priest is called to engage the world in which he lives, and the culture itself will provide the creativity for his sermons, teachings, and bulletins. In his journals, Schmemann frequently reflected on the current events of the day, always rooting them within the larger framework of the Gospel and salvation. At one point in his notes on pastoral theology, Schmemann remarks:

> But this is not merely a "knowledge in itself," but the communication of Truth to men and, therefore, the expression of this Truth in human words, categories, and thought forms. It is always related to culture and its goal is to "Church" the human mind, [to] illumine the whole of it with Divine Truth. This goal implies that a priest must know not only theology but culture as well, for his very function will be to relate God's truth to man's life. All the great Fathers of the Church were well instructed in the

---

11. Ibid.
12. Ibid.

"culture" of their time and it is evident that the proper understanding of Orthodox theology is simply impossible without good philosophical, historical, and literary preparation. One can memorize the catechism and the decisions of the Ecumenical Councils but unless one's mind is trained to understand them, this knowledge will remain dead and fruitless . . . Once more, the indifference of our Church to the intellectual content of the faith, its total concentration on the liturgical and practical aspects of Church life, is a dangerous trend and unless it is reversed quite soon, the very survival of Orthodoxy in a society which more than ever require[s] competence will become problematic.[13]

Practical Preparation

Furthermore, Schmemann identifies the need for the practical preparation of the priestly candidate. Practical preparation includes knowledge of the outline of forms and services, the customs and traditions, practice and conduct of the local Church administration—which includes keeping parish records, and maintaining correspondence with bishops and other priests—as well as the ability to perform marriages, funerals, and memorial services. This last element is especially important, as a congregation will themselves feel the tension and anxiety of a priest who does not feel comfortable serving at the altar.[14] This also extends to delivering homilies: If a priest is not well prepared, the congregation will certainly know. This does not mean that the priest has to be the perfect liturgical celebrant, but he really ought to have enough understanding of the rites and rituals to perform the liturgy in a way that is prayerful and smooth, and can be understood by his parishioners. Schmemann concludes by saying, "If experience comes only with life, one can avoid many mistakes and disappointments by being practically prepared for the salvation that awaits us."[15]

In Christ himself we have the perfect image of a priest: one who is pure, blameless, and righteous, who offers thanksgiving to God. The supreme example of prayer is Jesus' prayer to his Father in the Garden of Gethsemane to preserve unity and harmony among his disciples so that they can continue the ministry he began. In this,

---

13. Schmemann, "Notes on Pastoral Theology," Alexander Schmemann Collection, 9.

14. On more of the priestly nature of liturgy see Aidan Kavanagh, *Elements of Rite: A Handbook of Liturgical Style* (Collegeville, MN: Pueblo, 1982).

15. Schmemann, "Notes on Pastoral Theology," Alexander Schmemann Collection, 9.

Jesus completely and most perfectly expresses the priestly, kingly, and prophetic roles which all the baptized are called to emulate.

Ultimately, priestly service is a ministry of love, founded on Love itself, Jesus Christ, who was sent into this world in order to show us how to love, for our salvation. A priest cannot be a priest apart from love. His only example is Christ himself, who repeatedly demonstrates his long-suffering love through his acceptance of the stranger and outsider, through his miracles, through acts of kindness such as the washing of the feet of his disciples, and ultimately through the sacrifice of his own life on the cross. At Golgotha we see the greatest gift of love, the giving of oneself for the neighbor, a theme that comes up throughout the Scriptures. Golgotha is where Christ affirmed his role as the high priest for us, where the unblemished Lamb was slain. Christ became the high priest so that we could continue this priestly ministry from generation to generation, as expressed in the Eucharistic offering. It is here in the Eucharist that the entire Church, clergy and laity, is seen side by side, fulfilling their priestly roles in different ways. The same Eucharist provides us with a lens through which we can re-envision pastoral care for the contemporary Church. We will first look at the theological foundations of the sacrament before entering into the rite of the Eucharist, continuing to use Alexander Schmemann as our guide.

Part III

Eucharist as
Fulfillment of
Pastoral Theology

Chapter 8

Theological Foundations of the Eucharist

A Tour of the Divine Liturgy

Throughout his writings, Schmemann returns to the theme of the Eucharist again and again. Even the personal commentaries by his wife Juliana about their attendance at the small early morning liturgies at St. Serge seminary in Paris reflect Schmemann's love for the Eucharist.[1] He often makes mention in his *Journals* of a particular festal liturgy at the seminary, or of serving liturgy at a local parish with a former student when he was on the road.[2] His life revolved around the Church year; the feasts and fasts, especially Holy Week and Easter, were a major part of who Schmemann was and what he stood for. Furthermore, Schmemann saw the Eucharistic liturgy not just as a sacrament that the Church celebrated but a sacrament that "actualizes" the Church or makes it present, makes it real to us. To Schmemann, the Eucharist is the revelation of the Kingdom of God. The Eucharist is also where we see the fulfillment of our Baptism and our consequent roles in the royal priesthood of the Church. If one wants to see the foundation of ministry, one must always look to the Eucharist.

The Divine Liturgy is the major Eucharistic service in the Eastern Orthodox liturgical tradition. It is in the Divine Liturgy—generally just called liturgy—that the faithful gather together in order

---

1. Elena Silk, "The Eucharistic Revival Movement in the Orthodox Church in America: Past, Present, and Future." MDiv. thesis located at the Father Georges Florovsky Library of St. Vladimir's Orthodox Seminary, 1986, 26.

2. See Alexander Schmemann, *The Journals of Father Alexander Schmemann, 1973–1983* (Crestwood, NY: St. Vladimir's Seminary Press, 2000), 72, 105, 127, 131, 155, and 167.

to celebrate the Lord's Death and Resurrection. The overall sense of worship can be likened to a symphony, in that all the parts, including the congregation, work together in harmony, offering their prayer and praise to God. Liturgy requires active participation by the entire congregation, clergy and laity, which is even noted in the prayer books. Even the word *liturgy* is a witness to this, as it literally means "the work of the people." In antiquity, the term liturgy referred to something very much like modern-day public work projects. Therefore, on Sunday, we gather for the common or public work of the faith community: offering the holy Eucharist and sharing our fellowship in Christ with one another.

The major petitions are recited by the priest or deacon, and the people make a response such as: "Lord have mercy," "Grant it O Lord," or "Amen." In this way, the entire congregation offers one common prayer to God. It is easy to observe that an Orthodox liturgy is very active: The *a capella* choir responds to the petitions offered from the sanctuary; people come in and out of the congregation to light candles or say a prayer for a loved one; the Gospel book and the censer are processed around the church. Orthodox worship is full of movement. A colleague of mine referred to the liturgy as divine dance. I like that analogy.

Orthodox worship is also sensual, in that it appeals to the senses of sight, smell, taste, and hearing. The walls are decorated with multicolored icons. The deacon or priest processes through the Church swinging a bell-laden censer as gray smoke wafts through the air. The choir and readers sing or chant verses from Scripture. And of course the faithful come and partake of the Body and Blood of our Lord at Communion. The whole body is somehow taking part in this one common prayer to God. Orthodox worship is often called "traditional" because the priest still wears Byzantine- or Russian-style vestments, the singing is still done in an *a capella* style, and the clergy use incense at specific times during the services. The singing, combined with the use of images and incense, lends a mystical or spiritual quality to worship that many people consider "otherworldly" or "heavenly."

For centuries, Orthodox Christians have gathered together for the Divine Liturgy both as a way to share the joy and celebration with one another, and to offer their thanksgiving to God. It is this service of thanksgiving, translated by the word Eucharist, that is offered "for

the life of the world."[3] It is the Eucharistic liturgy to which
Schmemann devoted his entire life, as is especially seen in his book
The Eucharist.

Though it was published posthumously, *The Eucharist* was one
of Schmemann's most influential books. Throughout his journals, he
comments that writing this book—which took him nearly ten years to
finish—not only brought him great pleasure, but also allowed him to
synthesize his thoughts on the centrality of the Eucharist in the life of
the Church. This text is certainly the culmination of his life's work, as
echoes of many previous writings can be seen throughout the book.
When reading Schmemann's entire corpus, it may be tempting to say
that he repeats himself. However, a closer read of his writings reveals
very different approaches to theology and the liturgy. All of liturgy
inspired and influenced Schmemann, and therefore many aspects of
the liturgy became topics for his essays, books, and sermons. It's not
that he was repeating himself; rather, he was focusing on different
aspects of the liturgy at different times of his life. That is to say, *The
Eucharist* is not a mere repetition of Schmemann's thoughts about the
Eucharist; on the contrary, it provides an organic vision, explanation,
and synthesis of the Eucharistic liturgy, connecting the theology of
the Church with everyday life. Since he envisioned the liturgy as
deeply pastoral, Schmemann saw the liturgy—including the prayers,
liturgical seasons, feasts, and fasts—as having an important impact
upon pastoral theology. Schmemann also considered a wide variety of
topics that impacted the Church by hindering ecclesial life, like the
abuse of power in the Church and rampant clericalism already discussed, as well as a secularist worldview. Schmemann saw the answer
to these problems when he reflected upon the Eucharist. The
Eucharistic liturgy, which joins all these themes together, was not
only Schmemann's primary focus in his life and work, but is central
to theology and the Christian faith:

> For more than thirty years I have served the Church as a priest and a
> theologian, as a pastor and a teacher. Never in those thirty years have I
> ceased to feel called to think about the eucharist and its place in the life
> of the Church. Thoughts and questions on this subject, which go back to

---

3. *The Divine Liturgy According to St. John Chrysotom*, 2nd edition (South Canaan, PA:
St. Tikhon's Seminary Press, 1977), 64.

early adolescence, have filled my whole life with joy—but, alas, not only with joy. For the more real became my experience of the Eucharistic liturgy, the sacrament of Christ's victory and of his glory, the stronger became my feeling that there is a Eucharistic crisis in the Church. In the tradition of the Church nothing has changed. What has changed is the perception of the eucharist, the perception of its very essence. Essentially, this crisis consists in a lack of connection and cohesion between what is accomplished in the eucharist and how it is perceived, understood, and lived. To a certain degree this crisis has always existed in the Church. The life of the Church, or rather of the people of the Church, has never been perfect, ideal. With time, however, this crisis has become chronic. That schizophrenia that poisons the life of the Church and undermines its very foundations has come to be seen as a normal state. [4]

This crisis had previously been observed by Kern, who also noted that the Eucharistic liturgy had been diminished in popular piety, "The Eucharist was the basis and culmination of all liturgical life. But gradually everything that was concentrated around the Eucharist as the center of liturgical life—the Sacraments, prayers, orders of services . . . were turned in the consciousness of Christians into private rites, became the private business of each individual person or family, having (apparently) nothing to do with the concept of the gathered community." [5] We have to remember that both Kern and Schmemann lived at the beginning of this Eucharistic and liturgical renaissance, which placed the Eucharist in the center of their reflections. Afanasiev and Kern looked to the Eucharist as the source and summit of our life in Christ, to which everything in ecclesial life is connected. Schmemann built upon Kern's thought about this individual or private piety toward the Eucharistic liturgy and rites, as Kern had been in favor of understanding the liturgy as a Eucharistic gathering, reflecting its communal nature and its ties to the earliest of Christian traditions:

> This gathering is Eucharistic—its end and fulfillment lies in its being the setting where the "Lord's supper" is accomplished, wherein the Eucharistic "breaking of bread" takes place. In the same epistle St. Paul reproaches the Corinthians for partaking of a meal other than the Lord's supper in their gathering, or assembling for a purpose other than the Eucharistic

---

4. Schmemann, *The Eucharist*, 9.

5. Schmemann, *Introduction to Liturgical Theology* (Crestwood, NY: St. Vladimir's Seminary Press, 1997), 23.

breaking of bread (11:20-22ff). Thus, from, the very beginning we can see an obvious, undoubted tri-unity of the *assembly*, the *eucharist*, and the *Church*, to which the whole early tradition of the Church, following St. Paul, unanimously testifies.[6]

In order to better understand Schmemann's vision of the Eucharist, it is helpful to review his thoughts by looking at his own writing, and thus allowing Schmemann's voice to be heard in the Church today.

Schmemann divides *The Eucharist* into twelve chapters, each of which centers upon a different aspect of "sacrament," the theme that serves as a unifying thread for the entire text. The chapter titles—The Sacrament of the Assembly, The Sacrament of the Kingdom, The Sacrament of Entrance, The Sacrament of the Word, The Sacrament of the Offering, The Sacrament of the Anaphora, The Sacrament of Thanksgiving, The Sacrament of Remembrance, and The Sacrament of the Holy Spirit—reflect the idea of a journey to the Kingdom as well as the anticipation and fulfillment expressed in the Eucharistic liturgy. Furthermore, Schmemann understands the Eucharist as the unifying force in the Church. It is the focus for everything that is accomplished in the Church, especially meetings, social activities, committees, construction, fundraising and building campaigns, outreach and evangelism programs, and child and adult religious education programs. This unifying nature of the Eucharistic liturgy was a topic for reflection in Schmemann's journal in early 1973:

> The Eucharist reveals the Church as community—love for Christ, love in Christ—as a mission to turn each and all to Christ. The Church has no other purpose, no "religious life" separate from the world. Otherwise the Church would become an idol. The Church is the home each of us leaves to go to work and to which one returns with joy in order to find life, happiness and joy, to which everyone brings back the fruits of his labor and where everything is transformed into a feast, into freedom and fulfillment, the presence, the experience of this "home"—already out of time, unchanging, filled with eternity, revealing eternity. Only this presence can give meaning and value to everything in life, can refer everything to that experience and make it full. "The image of this world is passing away." But only by passing away does the world finally become the

---

6. Schmemann, *Eucharist*, 11 (emphasis in original).

"World": a gift of God, a happiness that comes from being in communion with the content, the form, the image of that "World."[7]

Schmemann does not advocate that each section or part of the Eucharistic liturgy should be explained independently, rather, the entire service flows together in an organic whole.

He uses the image of "journey" as a metaphor to describe the Eucharistic service. The Eucharist is where earth and heaven meet, where the creature meets the Creator in the preaching of the Gospel and the partaking of Holy Communion: "The liturgy of the Eucharist is best understood as a journey or procession. It is the journey of the Church into the dimension of the Kingdom. We use this word 'dimension' because it seems the best way to indicate the manner of our sacramental entrance into the risen life of Christ."[8]

Observing that the Eucharistic liturgy provides the content and context for a unique vision of life centered around the Gospel, Schmemann identifies throughout *The Eucharist* deep pastoral connections that exist between the Eucharist and everyday life, much like he does in this journal entry from December 1973:

> The Church has been established in this world to celebrate the Eucharist, to save man by restoring his Eucharistic being. The Eucharist is impossible without the Church, that is, without a community that knows its unique character and vocation—to be love, truth, faith, and mission—all of these fulfilled in the Eucharist; even simpler, to be the Body of Christ.[9]

When people come together for the Eucharistic assembly, they are gathering as the Church. According to Schmemann, the Church is not the sum total of individual people or a special group or society, but a gathering of the people of God. He reminds his readers that the Greek word for Church is *ekklesia*, which means "called together" or "called apart" for a specific purpose. In Old Testament times, God's people Israel were considered the *ekklesia*, in that they were called apart from all nations in order to submit to God's commandments and to follow and obey his Law. The Church is the continuation of this Israel of God, those people called apart to follow Christ and serve his

---

7. Schmemann, *The Journals*, 25.

8. Alexander Schmemann, *For the Life of the Word: Sacraments and Orthodoxy* (Crestwood, NY: St. Vladimir's Seminary Press, 1979), 26.

9. Juliana Schmemann, *Journals*, 25.

holy will (see Gal 6:16). The purpose for the gathering is for worship, prayer, and to offer thanksgiving to God. Here Schmemann cites the words of the Apostle Paul in his letter to the Corinthians, "when you meet as a church . . ." (1 Cor 11:18). In other words, the gathering or the assembly on Sunday is not for reasons of individual piety or spirituality—not for one's own sake—but in order to gather as the Church community. Throughout the Scriptures God always deals with a community, be it Israel or the early Church. Schmemann emphasizes the communal nature of the gathering over the individuality of the people who come together. In other words, the focus is on the assembly of the community of faith who constitute the Church, rather than on the concerns and problems of individual persons.

Schmemann was also keenly aware of the practical and pastoral needs of the faithful regarding the necessity for liturgical education and catechesis. In many ways, *The Eucharist* was a way of fulfilling this need in the Church, providing future generations with a basic understanding of the communal and unifying nature of the Eucharistic liturgy.

Assembly, Kingdom, Entrance into the Pastoral Mystery

As we have seen, Schmemann begins *The Eucharist* with the theme of journey and procession. He points to the Eucharistic liturgy as a journey to the Kingdom of God. This journey or procession begins not at Church but at home, when families prepare themselves to go to church by getting dressed, brushing their teeth, getting in the car, and driving to the church building. One could add that every Sunday liturgy is a preparation for the following Sunday—we live our lives Sunday to Sunday, Eucharist to Eucharist, until our last days.

When the people come together for the assembly, they are truly gathering as the Church. The purpose for their gathering is to offer worship, prayer, and thanksgiving to God. The Eucharist is not about "my needs" or "my piety"; instead, the central focus is on the Kingdom of God.[10] His explanation may seem very one-sided, given

---

10. Schmemann, *The Eucharist*, 23.

that everyone has specific spiritual needs and concerns that are important; however, Schmemann is dealing with the overemphasis on the individual, who expects the Church to "fulfill their needs," whatever those may be.[11] Schmemann also repeats that the gathering is neither for the clergy alone nor for the laity alone, but for all the people of God together. The entire Church is set apart to be the people of God in order to offer their common prayer, blessing, and thanksgiving to the Lord, and ultimately to become the Eucharistic community.

People gather together to offer their prayer and supplication to the Lord, and this is accomplished when they gather together as the Church. Schmemann indicates joining the assembly as the first corporate liturgical act:

> When I say that I am going to church, it means I am going into the assembly of the faithful in order, together with them, to constitute the church, in order to be what I became on the day of my baptism—a member, in the fullest, absolute meaning of the term, of the body of Christ . . . I go to manifest and realize my membership, to manifest and witness before God and the world the mystery of the kingdom of God, which already "has come in power."[12]

While the primary meaning of Church is the gathering or the assembly of people, the secondary meaning generally refers to the church as a physical or geographic location, as in the phrase, "I am going to church this morning." Even the physical space and architectural structure of the church building reveals the nature of "gathering" or "assembly," reveals the "conciliar or sobornal character of the Eucharist,"[13] the gathering of all creation under the dominion of God. Historically the church was the *domus ecclesiae*, literally the "home of the Church": the site of the gathering of Christians and of the Eucharistic breaking of bread. The *sobor*, as Schmemann says, is the "gathering together [of] heaven and earth and all creation in Christ—which constitutes the essence and purpose of the Church."[14]

---

11. Ibid., 12.
12. Ibid., 23.
13. Ibid., 19.
14. Ibid.

STRUCTURE AND PURPOSE OF THE ICONOSTASIS IN THE CHURCH BUILDING

The iconostasis is a floor-to-ceiling wall or screen upon which icons are hung, and which physically separates the altar from the nave or the common space within the church building. In ancient times, the iconostasis was only a small railing or knee wall type of construction that gave people a sense of distance from the altar, nothing at all like the large structures seen today.

THE ROLE OF THE PRIEST IN THE LITURGY

The Eucharistic context mentioned above gives Schmemann some insight into the role of the priest in the liturgy and in the Church. He states that the priest is the image of the head of the Body, and presides over the Eucharistic assembly. He is able to make Christ present because he was ordained, set apart for this ministry, by the laying on of hands of the bishop, who himself comes from a long line of bishops whose ordination can be traced to the Apostles themselves.

Schmemann goes onto say, "The priest is neither a 'representative' nor a 'deputy' of Christ; in the sacrament he is Christ himself, just as the assembly is his body. Standing at the head of the body, he manifests himself in the unity of the Church, the oneness of the unity of all her members with himself. Thus, in this unity of the celebrant and the assembled is manifested the divine-human unity of the Church—in Christ and with Christ."[15]

The reason for the gathering of the people of God is the common journey to the Kingdom, where the faithful are given the food and drink of eternal life. The reality of the Eucharist is the sacramental presence of God's Kingdom, which refers to the present moment as well as to the future:

> A sacrament is both cosmic and eschatological. It refers at the same time to God's world as he first created it and to its fulfillment in the kingdom of God. It is cosmic in that it embraces all of creation, it returns it to God as God's own—"Thine own of Thine own . . . on behalf of all and for all"—and in and by itself it manifests the victory of Christ. But it is to the

---

15. Schmemann, *The Eucharist*, 25.

same degree eschatological, oriented toward the *kingdom which is to come* . . . For if, as we have just said, the eucharist is the sacrament of the beginning and the end, then it is completed by the Church's ascent to heaven, to the "homeland of the heart's desire," the *status patriae*—the messianic banquet of Christ, in his kingdom. [16]

He then notes how the ideas of the sacramental nature of the Church and the Eucharist as constituting the Church run contrary to the typical "school theology," which reduces the Church to an administrative body or an institution that merely dispenses grace via the seven sacraments. In contrast, the Eucharist forms or constitutes the Church every time a liturgical gathering takes place. While on the one hand this gathering refers to the present age, it also points to the eschatological age, or the age of the Kingdom. This twofold reference is revealed in the liturgy, especially in its opening phrase, "Blessed is the kingdom of the Father and of the Son and of the Holy Spirit." [17] The focus is on the Kingdom of God and the journey that will soon take place. Schmemann comments:

> What does it mean to *bless* the kingdom? It means that we acknowledge and confess it to be our highest and ultimate value, the object of our desire, our love and our hope. It means that we proclaim it to be the goal of the sacrament—of pilgrimage, ascension, entrance—that now begins. It means that we must focus our attention, our mind, heart and soul, i.e., our whole life, upon that which is truly the "one thing needful." Finally it means that now, already in "this world," we confirm the possibility of communion with the kingdom, of entrance into its radiance, truth and joy. Each time that Christians "assemble as the Church," they witness before the whole world that Christ is King and Lord, that his kingdom has already been revealed and given to man and that a new and immortal life has begun. [18]

Schmemann therefore envisions the Church as the gathering of the people of God in order to offer praise and worship to God. This gathering incorporates everyone, adults and children, men and women, clergy and laity; all are gathered together in order to "become

---

16. Ibid., 34, 36 (emphasis in original).

17. *The Divine Liturgy According to St. John Chrysotom*, 2nd edition, 29.

18. Schmemann, *Eucharist*, 47–48 (emphasis in original).

the Church of God." As discussed above, this is a real concelebration, since everyone is gathered together around the Lord's table.

As we gather together each Sunday to celebrate the Eucharist, the entire Church offers up our common prayer, praise, and thanksgiving to God. While it is the priest who stands at the holy altar, offering the Eucharist on behalf of the community, it is the entire congregation that offers it. Schmemann emphasizes that though the priest is the liturgical celebrant and chief administrator of the parish, he is first and foremost one of the baptized members of the royal priesthood. As we look further at the liturgical rite of the Eucharist, we will see how Schmemann envisions our common celebration of this sacrament of the Kingdom.

Chapter 9

Eucharist in the Eastern Church

Word, Faith, Offering, Unity

The rites of the Eucharist in both the East and the West have a long historical development complete with many changes. However, as in his discussion of other sacraments, Schmemann is far less concerned with historical development than with what the Eucharist means. Since this book is primarily concerned with pastoral theology, we will follow Schmemann's lead, and discuss the received rite of the Eucharist as it is practiced in many Orthodox Churches today. When we examine the rite of the Eucharist, we see the fulfillment of Baptism in the common prayers of the people, in the listening to the Scripture readings, and in the offering of the Body and Blood of Christ. The Eucharist reveals the common work of the assembly, as examined in the previous chapter.

Following the initial gathering of the assembly, the people hear the proclamation of the Gospel and the preaching of the sermon or Homily. In the Eastern Orthodox liturgical tradition there are two prescribed Scripture readings during the liturgical gathering: one from a Pauline epistle and one from a Gospel. In the Roman Catholic Church, there are three prescribed readings on Sundays and solemnities. The Scripture readings and Homily are a vital part of the Eucharistic liturgy, since it is through the proclamation of God's Word that Christ is formed in the community. The community is presented with Jesus himself, rather than mere information about him; this deep connection between God's Word and our Christian life is noted in the prayer before the Gospel, which the priest prays at every liturgy:

Illumine our hearts, O master who loves mankind, with the pure light of
Thy divine knowledge. Open the eyes of our mind to the understanding
of Thy gospel teachings. Implant also in us the fear of Thy blessed commandments, that, trampling down all carnal desires, we may enter upon a
spiritual manner of living, both thinking and doing such things as are
well pleasing unto Thee. For Thou art the illumination of our souls and
bodies, O Christ our God, and unto Thee we ascribe glory, together with
Thy Father, who is from everlasting, and Thine all-holy, good, and life-
creating Spirit, now and ever and unto ages of ages. Amen.[1]

Schmemann points out that this division between the Liturgy of the
Word and Liturgy of the Sacrament is a false division, since there are
not two parts or halves of the liturgy but one unifying whole, and that
the entire service is sacramental: "Only in this unbreakable unity of
word and sacrament can we truly understand the meaning and
affirmation that the Church alone preserves the true meaning of
scripture. That is why the necessary *beginning* of the Eucharistic
ceremony is the first part of the liturgy—the *sacrament of the word*,
which finds its fulfillment and completion in the offering, consecration and distribution to the faithful of the Eucharistic gifts."[2]

    The prayers for the faithful and the entrance with the gifts
of bread and wine follow the Scripture readings and Homily.
Schmemann reflects on the Church as mission and prayer, as these
beautiful petitions and prayers reveal that the Church is alive, vibrant,
and organic.[3] The prayers for the faithful, together with the prayers
for the catechumens and the prayers before the Great Entrance, reveal
the cosmic quality of the Church. Here the Church prays for the sick
and suffering, for the military and armed forces, for those who are
living, and for those who are departed. The petitions reveal that the
Church is neither opposed to the world nor separate from it, but
rather called to encounter it. The prayers are comprehensive, and
the priest offers the names of everyone in the Church who is in
need of prayer. In these prayers, Church and world meet; to each,
the people respond, "Lord have mercy," "Grant it, O Lord," or

---

1. *Divine Liturgy of St. John Chrysostom Second Edition* (South Canaan, PA, 1979), Prayer
before the Gospel, 41.

2. Alexander Schmemann, *The Eucharist* (Crestwood, NY: St. Vladimir Seminary Press, 2003),
69 (emphasis in original).

3. Schmemann, *The Eucharist*, 69–70.

"Amen." It is worth repeating that both the petitions and responses are public and the entire congregation is invited to pray them, thus underscoring our common ministry in the royal priesthood.

These prayers for the faithful, together with the prayers for the catechumens, reveal the missionary vision of the Church: "For the prayers for the catechumens are above all a liturgical expression of a fundamental calling of the Church—precisely *the Church as mission*. The Church came into the world as mission—'Go into all the world and preach the gospel to the whole creation' (Mk 16:15)—and cannot, without betraying her nature, cease to be mission."[4] The missionary nature of the Church is made explicit in the hymns and prayers of the Eucharistic service.

Schmemann continues his commentary with an explanation of the importance of offering and sacrifice to pastoral theology. In *The Eucharist*, he reminds the reader of the bold animal sacrifices that were common in the Old Testament and throughout history. However, Schmemann points out that none of the sacrifices enumerated in the Old Testament writings—the animal offerings, the sin offerings, the grain offerings—could bring about salvation and redemption, because the Israelites lived under the rule of the Law and under sin, and as they continued to live under the Law, they could never find redemption.[5] The author of the letter to the Hebrews speaks of the same reality: "Since the law has only a shadow of the good things to come, and not the very image of them, it can never make perfect those who come to worship by the same sacrifices that they offer continually each year. Otherwise, would not the sacrifices have ceased to be offered, since the worshipers, once cleansed, would no longer have had any consciousness of sins?" (Heb 10:1–2). Redemption and salvation could only be given by God himself, since "Only God can save—precisely *save*—us, for our life needs salvation, and not simply help. Only he can fulfil that concerning which all sacrifices remain an impotent plea, of which they were all expectation, prefiguration and anticipation. And he fulfills this in the ultimate, perfect and all-embracing sacrifice in which he gave his only-begotten Son for the salvation of the world, in which the Son of God, having become the Son of man, offered

---

4. Ibid., 87 (emphasis in original).
5. Ibid., 101–105.

himself as a sacrifice for the life of the world."[6] Salvation could only take place when God's only-begotten Son took on human nature—including human thoughts, feelings, dreams, and fears—and was crucified on the cross. In other words, salvation and redemption were brought about through Jesus' self-offering on the cross:

> In this sacrifice everything is fulfilled and accomplished. In it, above all, sacrifice itself is cleansed, restored and manifested in all its essence and fullness, in its preeternal meaning as perfect love and thus perfect life, consisting of perfect self-sacrifice: in Christ "God so loved the world that he gave his only Son," and in Christ man so loved God that he gave himself totally, and in this twofold giving nothing remains not given, and love reigns in all . . . Everything that man, consciously or unconsciously, in darkness, partially, distortedly, included in his sacrifices, everything that man hoped for from them, and all that "heart of man could not conceive," was fulfilled, perfected and granted *once*—once and for all—in this sacrifice of sacrifices.[7]

This sacrificial offering was performed once and for all by Jesus through his Crucifixion. Here Schmemann enters into an important discussion concerning the so-called clerical nature of sacrificial offering. The prevailing theory was that it was through clerical power and grace that the gifts are transformed into the Body and Blood of Christ, while the laity remained passive participants and merely received the grace from the priest. Schmemann identifies the reduction made by this approach to the Eucharistic liturgy and theology, "The conviction that the priest serves *on behalf of* the laity and, so to speak, *in their place* led to the conviction that he serves *for* them, for the satisfaction of their 'religious needs,' subordinate to their 'demand.'"[8] In the prayers for priestly ordination in the Orthodox Church, no mention is made of special graces or powers granted to the priest; rather, the prayers emphasize his role to preach and teach, to offer the spiritual sacrifice (Eucharist), and to baptize.

This reduction, as with the other reductions of which Schmemann speaks, is contrary to the message contained in the Eucharistic prayers and hymns, which reveal that the entire congregation

---

6. Ibid., 103–104.
7. Ibid., 104.
8. Ibid., 114.

offers the bread and wine "in behalf of all and for all."[9] The priest is the liturgical celebrant, and as celebrant it is he who leads the prayers and blessings during the liturgy and, on behalf of all the people present, offers the gifts. In other words, the priest does not offer the gifts for himself, but for everyone gathered together as Church: "The uniqueness of the ministry of the priest consists in that he is called and appointed in the Church, the body of Christ, to be the *image* of the Head of the body—Christ—and this means to be the one through whom the *personal* ministry of Christ is continued and realized."[10]

Jesus offered his sacrifice not for himself but for the whole world. The Crucifixion was in order to "draw everyone to himself" (Jn 12:32), including Jews and Gentiles, men and women, adults and children, and indeed all of creation. The Crucifixion is symbolic of unity and love. Schmemann says that this unity and love is expressed in the Eucharistic liturgy, especially in the "kiss of peace," where the people exchanged a kiss in order to share their common love in Christ. This ancient rite is not practiced in all liturgical traditions, and in others it is practiced only by the clergy, as in the Orthodox and Catholic liturgies of Schmemann's time; the Latin Rite has since restored it to the people, and in some Orthodox parishes today the parishioners are beginning to exchange the kiss of peace as well. Schmemann comments that this kiss of peace reminds those who are gathered together that the purpose of the Eucharist is love: "Thus, in the 'holy kiss' we express not our own love—rather, we embrace each other through the new love of Christ. And is this not the joy of communion, that I receive this love of Christ from the 'stranger' standing across from me, and he from me? And that in it we are both 'revealed' to each other as participants in Christ's love, and this means as *brothers in Christ?*"[11]

ANAPHORA, THANKSGIVING, REMEMBRANCE

Following the kiss of peace and the recitation of the Creed, the celebrant begins the recitation of the anaphora, sometimes referred to as the Eucharistic prayers. The anaphora prayers are considered the

---

9. *The Divine Liturgy According to St. John Chrysotom*, 2nd ed., 65.

10. Schmemann, *The Eucharist*, 116–117

11. Ibid., 139 (emphasis in original).

very core of the Eucharistic liturgy, and function as a recapitulation of
the story of salvation; they reveal the preparation of the divine
Incarnation through the sending of the Law and the Prophets, the
sending of the Son, and finally the giving of the Holy Spirit. These
prayers, whether in their shorter form in the liturgy of St. John
Chrysostom or in their longer form in the liturgy of St. Basil the
Great, emphasize the work of salvation and the bestowal of grace to
the people of God.

In this section of *The Eucharist*, Schmemann reflects on
theological questions rooted in the historical debates about the
transformation of the gifts of bread and wine into the Body and Blood
of Christ. He encourages theologians to focus not on technical
questions such as the exact moment of the transformation of the bread
and wine, but to reflect instead on the more "urgent" question of
"what is accomplished in the Eucharist."[12] This, Schmemann sees, is
the deeper and more important question. Even if one were to pinpoint
an exact moment when the gifts are transformed into the Body and
Blood of Christ, the entire Eucharistic liturgy can be seen as a pro-
gression or a journey, in which, just as the gifts are transformed, so
too are those assembled being continually transformed by the grace of
the Holy Spirit and through the reception of the Body and Blood of
Christ. In the Eastern Church, one could even say that there really is
not one specific point in time that the gifts are transformed, but that
through the entire liturgy the gifts are set aside for the use of the
congregation, are prayed over with our petitions and the proclamation
of the Word of God, and then the final anaphora prayers form the
culmination or affirmation of the transformation of the gifts.[13]

In this section Schmemann reminds his readers that at the
heart of the anaphora prayers is the theme of remembrance: the
remembrance of the Law and the Prophets, the remembrance of the
sending of the Son into the world, the remembrance of the Crucifixion
and Resurrection, and even the remembrance of the glorious second
coming. The term remembrance, or *anamnesis*, refers to an eschatological remembrance, a personal making present of the remembered
event, rather than a mere recollection of a historical place and time.

---

12. Ibid., 163.
13. Ibid., 162.

This biblical understanding of *anamnesis* is connected to our remembrance of God and God's remembrance of us:

> The essence of our faith and the new life granted in it consists in *Christ's memory*, realized in us through our *memory of Christ*. From the very first day of Christianity, to believe in Christ meant to *remember* him and keep him always *in mind*. It is not simply to "know" about him and his doctrine, but to *know him*—living and abiding among those who love him. From the very beginning the faith of Christians was memory and remembrance, but memory restored to its lifecreating essence—for, as opposed to our "natural," "fallen" memory, with its illusory, "resurrection of the past," this new memory is a joyous recognition of the one who was resurrected, who lives and therefore is present and abides, and not only recognition but also encounter and the living experience of communion with him.[14]

This notion of remembrance, then, refers not so much to a historical event as to a present reality. When Jesus instructed his disciples to "do this in remembrance of me" at the Last Supper, he was not requesting a mere historical repetition, but was identifying that the memorial meal in which his followers would partake would be an important, salvific action, making present Jesus' very life. In other words, the weekly Eucharistic gathering of the people of God is both memorial and sacrifice; therefore this remembrance is not an individual or private concern, but the communal remembrance of the entire Church. Remembrance is a vital part of participation in the Eucharist service.

Schmemann further connects this remembrance to the knowledge of God. If one remembers a person or place, then one has knowledge of that person or place. This knowledge is not merely facts or data, but is connected to love. To "know" something or someone carries a connotation of intimacy and closeness; on their way to Emmaus after the Crucifixion, the disciples encountered the risen Lord and concluded, "Were not our hearts burning (within us) while he spoke to us on the way and opened the scriptures to us?" (Lk 24:32). Elizabeth Newman points out that intimate knowledge of and desire for God are the foundation for all theology, especially seen in the intimate and unifying nature of the Eucharist: "The metaphor of 'our hearts burning within us' is perhaps one of the best ways I know to describe theology as integral knowledge, as knowing internally

---

14. Ibid., 128–129. Note that Roman Catholic teaching holds that the transformation of the bread and wine is effected by the words of institution.

related not only to doing, but also related to our passions, desires, and in fact the very core of who we are continually called to be before God."[15] This intimate desire for the knowledge of God is explicitly inherent in the Eucharistic liturgy, upon which Schmemann comments:

> And thus, the Eucharist is also the sacrament of our access to God and knowledge of him and union with him. Being offered in the Son, it is offered to the Father. Being offered to the Father, it is fulfilled in the partaking of the Holy Spirit. And therefore the Eucharist is the eternally living and life-creating source of the Church's knowledge of the Most Holy Trinity. This is not the abstract knowledge (of dogmas, doctrine) that unfortunately remains for so many of the faithful, but knowledge as a genuine recognition, as meeting, as experience, and thus partaking of life eternal.[16]

Communion

If the Eucharist is the fulfillment of Baptism, then the fulfillment of the Eucharist is the reception of Holy Communion. The reception of Holy Communion is the affirmation and seal of one's membership in the Body of Christ. However, as Schmemann notes here and elsewhere, the reception of Holy Communion has often been regarded in recent centuries as an act of personal or individual piety and a special "means of grace," rather than the sign of one's membership in the Church. Schmemann considers this false understanding of Communion as contributing to a major "ecclesiological crisis" in the Church that has affected every generation in both the Eastern and Western Church.

Schmemann identifies the main factor contributing to the laity's infrequent reception of Holy Communion as a problem of personal "unworthiness." For many people, belief in their own sinfulness, combined with attempts at attaining "holiness"—such as extreme fasting, the recitation of preparatory prayers, or a "requirement" of Confession before each Communion—prevented them from approaching the chalice on Sundays or feast days. These

---

15. Elizabeth Newman, "Alexander Schmemann and Orthodox Theology: The Liturgy and Sacred *Sprachspiel.*" (Doctoral dissertation, Duke University, 1990), 191.

16. Schmemann, *The Eucharist*, 168.

individualistic exercises of pietistic attempts at becoming "worthy" have made frequent Communion nearly impossible for many Orthodox faithful. Thomas Hopko—former dean of St. Vladimir's Theological Seminary, pastor, and Orthodox theologian—has commented on the very stringent rules and regulations that have developed around the preparation and reception of Holy Communion. In the Orthodox response to the World Council of Churches' document *Baptism, Eucharist, and Ministry*, he discusses the vast gulf between frequent Communion, which was the traditional norm in antiquity, and the common contemporary practice of abstaining from Communion in many Orthodox Churches. In the essay, Hopko sketches a dim picture of this decline and many consequent abuses regarding the reception of Holy Communion among the Orthodox Christians in North America and throughout the world. In many traditional Orthodox communities, such as those in Greece, Russia, and former Eastern Bloc countries, as well as in some Orthodox communities in the United States and Canada, frequent Communion is not the norm.[17] The frequent reception of Communion did not become normative in the Orthodox Church in America until the Eucharistic revival that began in the 1960s and continues today.[18] This revival was led largely by the efforts of Schmemann, who saw the Eucharist as the central context of Church life, without which the Church would merely be an administrative institution with services, prayers, and blessings but without any reference to the Kingdom of God.

Schmemann's focus on the Kingdom and the Eucharistic nature of the Church is clearly connected to the reception of Communion. For Schmemann, Communion was not something that one received for "personal growth" or "sanctity," but rather a unifying symbol that connected the individual to Christ and to the Church.[19]

---

17. Even in my own pastoral experience I have encountered a few people who still do not receive Holy Communion even though it is offered every week. They were raised in an Orthodox tradition which put heavy emphasis on fasting for the entire week prior to the Sunday liturgy and confessing one's sins to a priest every Saturday evening.

18. See Silk, "The Eucharistic Revival Movement in the Orthodox Church in America." In his 1972 report to the Holy Synod of Bishops of the Orthodox Church in America, Schmemann bemoaned that the "questions and controversies" about frequent Communion still plagued the Church.

19. Schmemann, *Of Water and the Spirit* (Crestwood, NY: St. Vladimir's Seminary Press, 1979), 10.

In his 1972 report to the Holy Synod of Bishops of the Orthodox Church in America, Schmemann commented on the necessity of frequent Communion and its connection with membership in the Church:

> The early Church simply knew no other sign or criterion of membership but the participation in the sacrament. The excommunication from the Church was the excommunication from the Eucharistic assembly in which the Church fulfilled and manifested herself as the Body of Christ. Communion to the Body and Blood of Christ was a direct consequence of Baptism, the sacrament of entrance into the Church, and there existed no other "condition" for that communion. The member of the church is the one who is in communion with the Church in and through the sacramental communion, and thus one early liturgical formula dismissed from the gathering, together with the catechumens and the penitents, all those who are not to receive communion. This understanding of communion, as fulfilling membership in the Church can be termed *ecclesiological*. However obscured or complicated it became later, it has never been discarded; it remains forever the essential norm of Tradition.[20]

CONCLUSION

Schmemann's final book, *The Eucharist*, contains a synthesis of his thoughts and comments about the Eucharist as the sacrament of sacraments and a unifying symbol for Christians. The Eucharistic liturgy is not meant for passive participation; rather, the liturgy makes the Church what it is, the Body of Christ.

Schmemann's keen awareness of and sensitivity toward culture and society provided him with insight into the major problems of the Church, namely, secularism, clericalism, and the lack of a strong lay ministry. The gathering of the people of God around Word and table, and the reception of the Body and Blood of Christ, become the central symbol for the Christian life.

---

20. Schmemann, *Confession and Communion*, 3.

Conclusion

This book has highlighted Alexander Schmemann's distinctive theological contributions to pastoral theology within the Eastern Orthodox theological tradition. According to Schmemann, pastoral theology is rooted within the liturgical worship of the Church, most notably the Eucharistic gathering. It is within this context that the Church gathers together for prayer and to celebrate the Death and Resurrection of Jesus Christ.

Schmemann emphasized that pastoral theology was not a separate theological subject unto itself, but is rather the living expression, affirmation, and extension of liturgical worship. According to this sacramental approach, then, pastoral theology must be considered in relation to the liturgy of the Church, and must therefore be fully realized in the Eucharistic gathering, the Divine Liturgy.

Schmemann also maintained that pastoral ministry is not only for the ordained clergy, but for the entire people of God, both clergy and laity. This idea is not uniquely his, but is shared by many noteworthy theologians, mostly of the Paris School, including Afanasiev, Bulgakov, Kern, Kartashev, and Nikolai Berdyaev. Schmemann demonstrated that pastoral ministry is a participation in Christ's ministry, which is sacrificial in nature. Just as Christ offered himself as a living sacrifice, so too does the entire congregation, led by the priest, offer the Eucharistic liturgy "in behalf of all and for all."[1]

Schmemann identified Baptism and Chrismation (Confirmation) with entrance into the ministry of Christ's priesthood, and indicates the Eucharist as the fulfillment of both Baptism and Chrismation. Additionally, the clergy and the laity both share the pastoral vocation: to offer prayers and praise to God, and to live the life of the Gospel. However, the ordained priesthood has the additional specific function of leading the congregation in the Eucharistic liturgy.

A pastoral theology that is rooted within the liturgy of the Church may be an answer to the fundamental misunderstanding of

---

1. Ephesians 4:15.

ministry in the Church today. I noted earlier that within the academy
the prevailing model of priestly ministry is one of assisting parishioners
with their spiritual and social problems, rather than one of bringing
parishioners to a new relationship with the crucified and risen Lord.
Some schools of thought place more emphasis on the psychological
underpinnings of ministry than on the theological vision of pastoral
care. Schmemann's writings have greatly enhanced this new direction
of pastoral theology by emphasizing the sacramental nature of ministry. The priest is first and foremost the celebrant of the Eucharist,
leading the congregation in worship. He engages in his pastoral work
through the liturgical celebration, especially through regular preaching and teaching. However, the priest is also a man of prayer, leading
people in community prayer in addition to praying with the sick and
homebound, visiting those in prisons and hospitals, and assisting
those who are dying. Schmemann acknowledged the importance of
dealing with people's personal issues and spiritual problems. However,
the core of his thought remained sharply focused on the theology of
the Church.

Looking ahead, we might ask how we can change the current
direction of pastoral theology to one that mirrors the thought of
Schmemann and could be a corrective to the present misunderstanding
of pastoral theology in the academy. How can pastoral theology be
once again the center and focus of our seminary curricula, and how
can our seminaries once again foster and encourage good pastors to
serve our Church, equipping the laity for the building up of the Body
of Christ? Schmemann certainly saw the need for a liturgical renewal
and revival during his lifetime; now the Church is in the midst of a
theological desert when it comes to pastoral theology. If the academy
is really concerned about pastoral education and formation, then
changes need to be implemented in the way seminaries train and
educate future clergy.

A Challenge to the Academy

If the Church wants to flourish and grow into the image of the Lord
of all, then we must challenge our seminaries and theological academies to change the way in which pastoral formation is currently
practiced. We cannot wait; time is of the essence. The academy has

tried time and time again to equip students with new methods for evangelization, missionary work, and preaching; however, studying these subjects by themselves, in isolation, is detrimental to pastoral development. Schmemann reminds us that these theological areas find their context within the liturgical worship of the Church, around the Lord's table. Schmemann was clear: pastoral theology must be first and foremost a proclamation of the Kingdom of God through the preaching and teaching of the Gospel and through the sacraments of the Church.

Drawing from the lead of Alexander Schmemann, the academy would do well to turn to its rich and robust liturgical tradition to help equip the future leaders of the Church, especially those in priestly ministry and pastoral formation. The Church's worship—the Eucharist, sacraments, prayer services, blessings, and other rites—are the very foundation of pastoral ministry. If we follow the ancient saying of Prosper of Aquitaine, *lex orandi, lex credendi*, then we must return once again to worship to help us prepare the leaders of tomorrow. Future pastors will certainly encounter a variety of people, problems, and situations in their ministry, and they will turn to the liturgy for comfort and assistance. Their preaching will take place in the context of worship. Their teaching will be based on the Lectionary readings that follow the feasts and fasts of the Church; their bedside prayers in the hospital will come from the breviary. All of this points to the obvious: rather than looking to the "new and improved" methods of pastoral care, why not return to the timeless, ageless liturgical life of the Church?

Perhaps the academy will consult the writings of Alexander Schmemann as they begin to refocus their attention on pastoral theology and reform the way pastoral care is taught in seminaries and schools of theology. In doing so, they would allow Schmemann's prophetic voice to inspire a new generation of faculty and students to serve Jesus Christ and his Church in an ever-deeper way.

Index

ABOUT THE LITURGICAL INSTITUTE

The Liturgical Institute, founded in 2000 by His Eminence Francis
Cardinal George of Chicago, offers a variety of options for education
in liturgical studies. A unified, rites-based core curriculum constitutes the foundation of the program, providing integrated and
balanced studies toward the advancement of the renewal promoted
by the Second Vatican Council. The musical, artistic, and architectural
dimensions of worship are given particular emphasis in the curriculum.
Institute students are encouraged to participate in its "liturgical
heart" of daily Mass and Morning and Evening Prayer. The academic
program of the Institute serves a diverse, international student
population—laity, religious, and clergy—who are preparing for service in parishes, dioceses, and religious communities. Personalized
mentoring is provided in view of each student's ministerial and profes-
sional goals. The Institute is housed on the campus of the University
of St. Mary of the Lake/Mundelein Seminary, which offers the
largest priestly formation program in the United States and is the
center of the permanent diaconate and lay ministry training programs
of the Archdiocese of Chicago. In addition, the University has the
distinction of being the first chartered institution of higher learning
in Chicago (1844), and one of only seven pontifical faculties in
North America.

For more information about the Liturgical Institute and its programs,
contact: usml.edu/liturgicalinstitute. Phone: 847-837-4542. E-mail:
litinst@usml.edu.

Msgr. Reynold Hillenbrand
1904-1979

Monsignor Reynold Hillenbrand, ordained a priest by Cardinal George Mundelein in 1929, was Rector of St. Mary of the Lake Seminary from 1936 to 1944.

He was a leading figure in the liturgical and social action movement in the United States during the 1930s and worked to promote active, intelligent, and informed participation in the Church's liturgy.

He believed that a reconstruction of society would occur as a result of the renewal of the Christian spirit, whose source and center is the liturgy.

Hillenbrand taught that, since the ultimate purpose of Catholic action is to Christianize society, the renewal of the liturgy must undoubtedly play the key role in achieving this goal.

Hillenbrand Books strives to reflect the spirit of Monsignor Reynold Hillenbrand's pioneering work by making available innovative and scholarly resources that advance the liturgical and sacramental life of the Church.